STRANGE

STRANGER GOD

MEETING JESUS IN DISGUISE

RICHARD BECK

FORTRESS PRESS

MINNEAPOLIS

Be not forgetful to entertain strangers:
for thereby some have entertained
angels unawares.

—Hebrews 13:2 (KJV)

CONTENTS

INTRODUCTION:
WELCOMING THE
STRANGER GOD

God, the Bible tells us, comes to us in strangers. And as Jim Morrison of the Doors sang, people are strange. Strangers, I guess, are especially so—which makes it hard for us to welcome the stranger God.

If I may start with a strange story, let me tell you why the man in the cell next to Mr. Albert was drinking out of his toilet.

I tend to call Al "Mr. Albert," because he is older than I am and I'm a sucker for Southern manners. I'll add Mr. or Miss to your name if you're my senior. Mr. Albert has been in prison for a few decades, and he's been a longtime member of the Bible class I teach each week at the maximum-security French Robertson Unit just north of my hometown in Abilene, Texas. I've been going out to the prison for over five years now, every Monday night.

Back when I was doing the chaplaincy training

to get clearance to lead the Bible study, the head chaplain asked me why I wanted to come out to the prison.

"Matthew 25," I answered, "Jesus said we'd find him disguised as a prisoner. So I'm out here looking for Jesus."

This is a book about Matthew 25—about how Jesus comes to us in disguise, in foreigners and refugees, in the homeless and the outcasts, in the prisoner and the hungry. This is a book about the strangeness of a God who comes to us in strangers. In the parable of the Sheep and the Goats, Jesus is disguised as the prisoner and the sick. In your life, Jesus might be disguised as the coworker at the watercooler or the Muslim woman standing next to you in the grocery store.

This is a book about the ancient Christian practice of hospitality, about encountering the God who surprises us in strangers. Do not forget to practice hospitality, the book of Hebrews entreats us, for some of us have entertained angels unawares.

True, the Men in White in the prison (inmates in Texas wear all white) and Mr. Albert are unlikely angels: I'd never imagined angels could have that many tattoos. But over and over again, Jesus has kept his promise and come to me in the Men in White.

Which brings me back to Mr. Albert's story.

Al had been put into Ad Seg, which stands for Administrative Segregation—it's the jail within the prison, solitary, the hole. A prisoner is in a cell all by himself and cannot leave it for twenty-three hours of the day. Most of the men in Ad Seg are there because they are extraordinarily violent, but you're also sent to Ad Seg as punishment.

Mr. Albert sat alone in Ad Seg in a cell that had dried feces smeared on the walls. But what really was gnawing at him wasn't disgust or loneliness; it was the injustice that had befallen him. Al had been accused by the guards of something he didn't do, landing him in Ad Seg. So while Al sat in that disgusting cell, his hatred for the guards boiled and seethed.

As the days passed in Ad Seg, Al got to talking with the inmate in the cell next to his. The sink wasn't working in the man's cell, so when he grew thirsty, he had to drink the water out of the cell's toilet. Many times, the man had asked for his sink to be repaired, but the guards didn't listen. So the man kept drinking out of the toilet.

Feeling sympathy for his fellow prisoner, Al would take a scrap of plastic and fill it with water from his sink. He'd then tie it off, making a small, improvised water balloon. Al would slide the balloon down the hallway toward the door of the man's cell. The man would reach out and grab the water balloons. Thanks to Al, he could drink the water from these water balloons rather than from the toilet.

Al eventually got out of Ad Seg, but his anger and hate for the guards lingered. A spiritual poison was seeping through his heart and soul.

And then things got worse.

Al received a call from his daughter. She was engaged, she announced, and the couple had set a date. While Al and his daughter rejoiced together, they also cried because Al couldn't be there to walk her down the aisle and give her away on her wedding day.

All this sent Al into a deeper spiritual pit. The injustice of his time in Ad Seg, the inability to walk his daughter down the aisle—it was all too much.

On the day of the wedding, a guard approached Al. "Come with me," the guard said. Al got up and followed.

The guard led Al to an office with a phone. "You can pick it up," the guard said.

Al picked up the line and said hello.

The voice of his daughter answered.

The timing of the call had been arranged by the guards. Al's daughter was standing at the back of the church, and the wedding march was about to play.

The call had been organized so that Al could speak to his daughter right before she walked down the aisle.

Al had tears in his eyes at the Bible study one Monday night, when he shared this story of his journey through darkness into this unexpected moment of grace.

"Satan will tell you lies," Al said, "Lies that these guards are evil and that nothing good is in them. I believed those lies for a very long time. But I'm here to tell you that there is good in everyone. The phone call with my daughter showed me that."

Over and over again, Jesus comes to us in disguise. Jesus comes to the man in Ad Seg as his neighbor slides him water balloons. Jesus comes to Mr. Albert in the guards who arrange the phone call with his daughter on her wedding day. Jesus comes to me everywhere in the testimony Al shared that night in our Bible study, in Al's humanity to the man in Ad Seg, in the surprising act of kindness from the guards, in Al's tear-filled testimony of confession, repentance, and forgiveness. I came to the prison looking for Jesus, and I found him.

Yet, over and over, we miss seeing Jesus. The very people Jesus names in Matthew 25—the prisoner, the homeless, the hungry—are named precisely because we *don't* see them. The parable of the Sheep and the Goats in Matthew 25 is a cautionary tale. In the parable, all of humanity stands before the judgment seat of God. God sends some to the left, the goats, and some to the right, the sheep. After the sorting, God says to the goats, "Depart from me, you who are cursed, into the eternal fire prepared for the devil and his angels. For I was hungry and you gave me nothing to eat, I was thirsty and you gave me nothing to drink, I was a stranger and you did not invite me in, I needed clothes and you did not clothe me, I was sick and in prison and you did not look after me." Alarmed and confused, the goats exclaim, "Lord, when did we see you hungry or thirsty or a stranger or needing clothes or sick or in prison, and did not help you?" Jesus's response, in a nutshell: "Everywhere. You saw me everywhere. I was standing right in front of you."

We know that God comes to us in strangers. We know there are angels out there. We know Jesus shows up in the very people we are overlooking or ignoring. Yet we end up acting like the goats in Matthew 25.

There's a simple answer for why we do this: Strangers are strange. *And that makes God strange.*

The etymological roots of the word *strange* go back to an Old French word *estrange*, meaning foreign, alien, unusual, and unfamiliar. Strangers are foreign to us, weird and unfamiliar, making us hesitant and even suspicious. Strangers take us out of our relational comfort zone. Consequently, the God who comes to us in strangers makes us feel anxious and awkward.

We know that the people of God are called to be a people of hospitality. Leviticus 19:34 commands, "The foreigner residing among you must be treated as your native-born. Love them as yourself, for you were foreigners in Egypt." Paul tells the church in Romans 12:13 to "practice hospitality." But the strangeness of strangers makes hospitality hard. As we've watched cable news and our social-media feeds, we've all witnessed our failures in extending hospitality to strangers, our unwillingness to welcome people into our nation, neighborhoods, schools, workplaces, churches, homes, and hearts. The refugee family stopped at our borders. The homeless person sleeping on our streets. The racial segregation that continues to plague our cities, schools and churches. The signs saying, "God Hates Fags." The nastiness of our political debates. And far too often, Christians have been the worst offenders, the very first to greet strangers with Keep Out signs. The God who comes to us in strangers is too strange for us to see. Like the goats in Matthew 25, we refuse to welcome Jesus in disguise.

As a psychologist, I'm frequently invited to work with groups and organizations who are passionate about welcoming strangers into their community. Many of us are working hard to extend a welcome across the social divides that separate us in the world, the big divides that dominate our news and social-media feeds—the racial, economic, and political divides and a host of other divides as well—all the big and little things that cause us to avoid and exclude each other. As I've visited and worked with these groups, I've found that while we often start with good intentions, initiatives, and mission statements, our plans struggle to get off the ground. To be sure, there are always a few passionate and devoted people who throw themselves into this work, but the work of welcoming strangers rarely becomes infectious and contagious. Good-hearted people, even committed followers of Jesus, continue to hold back. We know we're called to hospitality, but something keeps breaking down.

We fail at hospitality because hospitality doesn't begin with a program, with a new "welcoming" or "neighboring" initiative. Hospitality has to begin in the heart. The same goes for matters of law and policy. When we fear strangers, we erect walls and obstacles to keep them out. On social media and cable news, we fixate on the physical, legal, and economic walls that shut strangers out. But we routinely fail to notice that these external walls originate with *a failure of the heart*, with a wall erected within our souls.

This fear of strangers is called xenophobia, a word that combines the Greek word for stranger —*xenos*—with *phobia*, the word for fear. As the Doors sang, people are strange, and strangeness creates in us discomfort, anxiety, fear, and uneasiness around strangers.

By contrast, the biblical word for hospitality is *philoxenia*. *Philia*, you probably know from the city Philadelphia, is the Greek word for brotherly love. Hospitality begins in the heart. Instead of *phobia*, Christians are called to extend *philia* to strangers. So the central argument of this book is that hospitality—welcoming God in strangers and seeing Jesus in disguise—begins by widening the circle of our affections, the circumference of our care, the arena of our compassion, and the territory of our kindness.

But hearts aren't easily changed. You can't change hearts with pep talks, protests, podcasts, Facebook rants, tweets, or a really good sermon. Hearts require spiritual formation through habits and practices that directly address the social and psychological dynamics at work that keep us from seeing and welcoming each other. Some of these dynamics are social in nature, involving the way one demographic group feels about another demographic group: black versus white, rich versus poor, male versus female, straight versus gay, Democrat versus Republican, American versus people from any other country, citizen versus immigrant, Christian versus Muslim, and on and on. But many of the dynamics that separate us are personal and emotional in nature, reflecting how individuals are uniquely wired to push some people away and welcome others. The way we're wired—what we find scary, unpleasant, difficult, or strange in others— affects how welcoming we are and how hard or easy it is for us to see Jesus in a prisoner or in a homeless person, a political opponent, a refugee, or a coworker.

What gets ignored in the call for hospitality are these personal and emotional responses we have toward others. The God who comes to us in strangers is strange. And that strangeness trips us up, emotionally and interpersonally. Our discomfort causes us to hesitate and hold back. *Philia* gets trumped by *phobia*. We find ourselves leaning away from people rather than leaning in.

So hospitality demands more than good will and good intentions. Emotions, including social emotions, are not easily changed. You can't fix depression by telling someone, "Cheer up!" You can't get someone to become less angry just by admonishing, "Calm down" or less anxious by saying, "Don't worry, be happy!" Emotions can't be turned on or off like a light switch. The same goes for our feelings about people. Hospitality is an emotional battleground. If someone is scared about going into a prison, telling her, "Don't be scared" isn't helpful. The same goes for any other social group you find scary or suspicious. If you find some people irritating, annoying, or revolting, a demand that you should feel differently isn't practical. Yet these are the very feelings that cause us to miss seeing the God who comes to us in strangers.

These social feelings were at work in every part of Mr. Albert's testimony that night at the prison. Feelings of distrust and suspicion isolate the inmates from each other. Kindness is often interpreted as weakness, a vulnerability to be exploited. So Al sharing water with his neighbor was an unexpected act of grace, Jesus coming to an Ad Seg inmate in a stranger. Those same feelings of distrust and suspicion separate the guards and the inmates. A tense and often hateful relationship exists between the officers and the Men in White. Yet God surprises Al by coming to him in the guise of a guard, in the gift of the wedding-day phone call. And as scary as prisons and tattooed inmates might be, Jesus comes to me in Mr. Albert and the Men in White.

There are two big missing pieces in our efforts to welcome the stranger God. The first missing piece is that hospitality, before it can be anything else, begins as the emotional battle to widen the circle of our affections. Theologian Miroslav Volf calls this "the will to embrace."[1] But cultivating the will to embrace is hard, emotional work. The emotional barriers that separate us are formidable and difficult to overcome. That brings us to the second missing piece: that hospitality begins as a spiritual discipline, as a habit-forming practice aimed at expanding the bandwidth of our kindness and compassion. Our emotions change when we begin to adopt practices that slowly, over time, reconfigure our feelings and affections. A spiritual discipline that can do this for us is known as the Little Way of Saint Thérèse of Lisieux.

I've come to think of Thérèse's Little Way as the lost spiritual discipline. When we think of "spiritual disciplines," we think of practices like prayer, silence, solitude, Bible reading, Sabbath, and fasting. When we think of spiritual disciplines, we think of contemplative retreats in monastic settings. These

---

1. Miroslav Volf, *Exclusion and Embrace* (Nashville: Abingdon, 1996).

spiritual disciplines focus us on our relationship with God. Through spiritual disciplines, we seek a deeper intimacy with God, a greater awareness of God. We seek an encounter with the sacred and divine.

While these spiritual disciplines move us toward God, they routinely fail to move us toward each other. This is the genius of the Little Way, the lost spiritual discipline, a habit-forming practice that moves us toward each other so that our affections for each other expand and widen. The Little Way is a spiritual discipline of hospitality and welcome. This is exactly the practice we need if we want to overcome the strangeness of strangers, a habit-forming discipline that enables us to encounter the God who comes to us in disguise. The Little Way trains us to entertain angels unawares, God coming to us in coworkers, neighbors, refugees, the homeless, and the people in the line with us at the grocery store.

Even in cellmates, prison guards, and prisoners.

Matthew 25, the Parable of the Sheep and the Goats, doesn't have to be a cautionary tale for us. It doesn't matter what the Doors sing about people; we can learn to see Jesus in everyone.

That's the call to hospitality in a nutshell: welcoming the stranger God.

PART I

ENTERTAINING ANGELS

1

JESUS IN
DISGUISE

"Come inside," Robert invited. "I want you to see something."

I really didn't want to go inside. To be honest, Jesus doesn't often come to me in Robert. Plus, I've been in Robert and Judy's apartment a few times, and it's a big OCD trigger for me. The place is a mess, it has a foul odor, and there's pet hair everywhere. Robert and Judy almost got kicked out of the apartment a few months back because the HUD inspector said there was too much stuff in the apartment, making it a fire hazard.

But I took a deep breath and went inside.

Robert and Judy are friends from Freedom Fellowship, a mission church where my wife, Jana, and I share life with friends on the margins. Many of our friends at Freedom are poor and intermittently homeless. Many are on parole or struggling with addictions. Some, like Robert and Judy, have disability case workers and live in HUD housing.

Every week Jesus comes to me in my friends at Freedom, but not so much with Robert. Robert is hyper, talks too much and too loud, and is a bit of a know-it-all. Still, we're friends. And I absolutely love Judy, a simple and innocent soul. Every week after church, because the city buses have stopped running and most of our friends at Freedom don't own cars, I drive Robert and Judy home, along with Henry, Maria, and Josh. We're a motley crew, the six of us crammed into a car. But I look forward to our time together. Henry, Maria, and Josh are Hispanic, so my radio is tuned to 93.3 FM La Voz, a local Tejano station. We crank the tunes, and they educate me about Tejano music and teach me Spanish. We laugh a lot together.

Robert and Judy are the last to be dropped off. And one night, a few days before Christmas, Robert invited me in. "Come in, I want to show you something."

I didn't really want to see what Robert had to show me. The last time I was inside the apartment, I spent a frustrating hour trying to help Robert get a remote control synced with their TV. Robert can't read very well, so he needed me. But that didn't prevent him getting in my ear and telling me what to do every step of the way.

But Robert seemed really excited about what he wanted to show me. So I parked the car and followed them to their apartment.

We went inside, and the apartment was the way I remembered it: a mess.

Robert started upstairs and beckoned, "Come upstairs; it's upstairs."

In an effort to embody the Christmas spirit, I smiled and climbed the stairs. When I got to the room at the top, it was dark, and I couldn't see anything. "Wait here," Robert said. "Let me turn on the light." He crossed to the light and flipped the switch.

I blinked and took in the magical canopy that became illuminated above me.

It was stunning. I found myself in an enchanted fairyland. I don't know how long it took Robert to do it, but it was strange, beautiful, and mesmerizing. I was transfixed and at a loss for words.

For days and days, Robert had been tying a thread to every Christmas ornament he could find, and then he tied that string to a thumbtack that he pushed into the soft ceiling, hanging the ornament overhead. He had done this with hundreds of ornaments of all shapes, sizes, and colors. Wall to wall, the entire ceiling was a thick forest of twinkling light and color.

"How long did it take you to do this?"

"A long time," he beamed.

I stared, and walked around the room like a child looking up at a starry night sky. I wasn't sure what the HUD inspector was going to say when he got a look, but I knew what I thought as I walked under that magical Christmas canopy.

"It's beautiful, Robert," I said in a hushed voice.

"Merry Christmas, Richard," Robert said.

"Merry Christmas, Robert."

We smiled at each other under a sky of twinkling light.

And I was surprised all over again at how Jesus comes to me in disguise.

Hospitality Wars: Abraham versus Sodom

I went to the prison and Freedom looking for Jesus, and I found Jesus in Mr. Albert and Robert. Over and over, I've entertained angels unawares.

That encouragement in Hebrews is an echo of the primal story of hospitality in the Bible, the first story where we read about God being welcomed as a stranger. In Genesis 18, Abraham is sitting under a clutch of oak trees when three strangers approach. The strangers are collectively described as "the Lord." Seeing the strangers, Abraham jumps up and welcomes them, inviting them to sit under the shade of the oaks while a meal is prepared.

In church tradition, the three strangers called "the Lord" in Genesis 18 are often taken to be the members of the Trinity—Father, Son, and Holy Spirit. In the Eastern Orthodox tradition, where icons play an important part in worship and spiritual devotion, it is not allowed to paint God directly for fear of making a graven image. So the Orthodox iconographers paint God indirectly, by depicting this story of hospitality in Genesis 18 where God is welcomed as the stranger. The icons depicting this story are called "The Hospitality of Abraham," and the three visitors seated at Abraham's table are often called the Old Testament Trinity. The icon says it all: God is welcomed in extending hospitality to strangers.

That scene of hospitality in Genesis 18, where God is kindly welcomed, contrasts sharply with the events that transpire in the very next chapter. After the meal, two of Abraham's visitors go down to the towns of Sodom and Gomorrah on a reconnaissance mission to determine if the wickedness of the towns is as bad as it has been rumored. The visitors have a simple test: They plan to go to the center of the town and spend the night. How well will the city take care of the people sleeping on its streets?

Hospitality to strangers is God's test of goodness or wickedness.

Upon hearing of this test to sleep on the streets, Abraham's nephew Lot fears for the safety of the visitors. Lot knows what sort of welcome awaits strangers in Sodom and Gomorrah, so Lot takes the strangers into his home. But it's too late. Word of the strangers has gotten around, and a violent mob descends on Lot's house and demands that the visitors be sent outside to be raped. Ultimately, the angelic strangers help Lot escape the angry and sex-hungry mob.

We often think that the sin of Sodom is homosexuality. But when contrasted with Genesis 18, we see the real point of the story: Abraham welcomes the strangers and shows hospitality; the citizens of Sodom do the opposite. *The sin of Sodom is the failure to show hospitality.* Sodom failed to welcome the God who came to them as a stranger.

JESUS WAS A REFUGEE

From Genesis 18 onward, God keeps showing up incognito.

In the New Testament, the Gospel of John describes the Incarnation as the Word becoming flesh and dwelling among us. I like how Eugene Peterson in *The Message* translates this text: "The Word became flesh and blood, and moved into the neighborhood." The stranger God forces you to be a better neighbor. Indeed, Jesus started out his life as a refugee. Fleeing Herod's persecution, Mary, Joseph, and Jesus fled Israel to live in Egypt as immigrants and foreigners. Jesus was that weird foreign kid sitting in the back of the classroom. Zechariah 7:10 says, "Do not oppress the widow or the fatherless, the foreigner or the poor," and now we see why. That refugee is Jesus. God comes to us as an immigrant speaking with an accent.

Another example is in Luke 24. It's after the resurrection, and two of Jesus's followers are walking toward the town of Emmaus, perplexed by the reports of Jesus's empty tomb. Then a stranger appears (spoiler alert: it's Jesus), but they don't recognize him. This time Jesus is, quite literally, a stranger. Jesus then explains to the disciples how the Scriptures foretold the death and resurrection of the Messiah. As the trio draws near to the village of Emmaus, the sun is setting, so the two disciples extend hospitality to the stranger, welcoming him into their home for shelter and a meal. During that meal, Jesus takes the bread and breaks it, and in that moment, in the breaking of the bread, they recognize him. It's Jesus!

We encounter the risen Lord when we break bread with strangers. I experience this every week at Freedom when we gather with friends and neighbors to share a meal before our Wednesday-night praise service. Jesus comes to me in the tears of Mr. John as he shares with me the pain of losing his wife. This happened years ago, but Mr. John experiences this loss afresh each day, as if it just happened. Mr. John has shared this story with me perhaps a hundred times, as he has, over and over again, with everyone else. He doesn't seem to remember that he's told us. Regardless, when we weep together, I am on holy ground.

Mr. John can crack me up as well. Once he had an accident in the bathroom, soiling his pants. He was devastated and embarrassed. As we talked with Mr. John, we worked hard to comfort him, pointing out how sometimes our bodies betray us and let us down. Eventually Mr. John calmed down. He collected himself and reached a spiritual perspective on the situation: "You know," he said, "it's better to make a mess in your pants than a mess in your heart." Amen to that! I laughed and heartily agreed. It's one of the most profound things I've ever heard. Don't make a mess in your heart! Jesus comes to me in these meals with Mr. John.

My favorite example of Jesus coming to us in disguise is in Matthew 18. The disciples are arguing who is to be the Big Boss of the kingdom, sitting at Jesus's right hand. Jesus takes a child and puts him in the midst of the bickering, power-hungry men. "Whoever welcomes this child," Jesus says, "welcomes me." Jesus comes to us disguised as a child, as one of those he calls "the least of these."

We often miss the power of what Jesus was doing when he set a child at the center of the disciples' attention, for we live in a child-centered world. Children are the focus of many of our concerns and affections. But that wasn't the case in Jesus's time and place. Men were at the center of first-century Middle Eastern culture. And around the men were the women. At the periphery were the children, marginalized and ignored.

So you can see the power of what Jesus was doing. He reaches to the edges of his society, bringing a marginalized person into the center; the ignored and dismissed are now in the spotlight, the focus of our care, affection, and attention.

Our response to the call of hospitality is to answer some simple questions: Who are the people on the periphery of my life? Who is that person at the far boundaries of my care and attention? Who is being ignored in my workplace and church? Who is marginalized in my neighborhood and nation?

Who would Jesus grab to place at the center of my attention?

Because when I welcome that person, says Jesus, I welcome him.

SAVED BY STRANGERS

I went looking for Jesus out at the prison and at Freedom because I was losing my faith. At the time, I was full of doubts and questions. God seemed distant. I rarely prayed. So when I answered the Men in White in those early weeks out at the prison, I was telling the truth. I came to the prison because I was looking for God. That answer highlights one of the temptations we face in the call to hospitality. When we listen to these stories of hospitality in the Bible, we often get the characters reversed. When I go to churches to talk about hospitality, it's easy for my audiences, as good Christian people, to think that when we show hospitality, we are being like Jesus. And no doubt we are. Jesus welcomed tax collectors, prostitutes, and sinners. We, as followers of Jesus, extend that same hospitality to the outcasts and sinners of our time and place.

But as these Bible stories show, we don't show hospitality to *be like* Jesus. We show hospitality to *welcome* Jesus. In Matthew 25, Jesus isn't the one doing the visiting. Jesus is the one being visited. In these stories, God isn't the host. God is the stranger. Hospitality isn't *being like* God but *welcoming* God into our lives. As Jesus says in the book of Revelation, "I'm standing at the door, knocking." Hospitality is opening the door to let Jesus in.

I wasn't bringing Jesus into the prison or to Freedom. Jesus was already there—in disguise, yes, but there. And so, with flagging faith, I set out to *welcome* the God who comes to us in strangers.

In my first weeks out at the prison, I had to choose the content of my study with the Men in White. As a skeptical, doubting Christian, I was drawn to the lament psalms. The cries of protest and anguish in these psalms of darkness spoke into my own anger and doubt. Where was God in this broken and messed-up world?

Planning my first prison study, I figured if anyone could identify with the cries of godforsakenness and desolation in the lament psalms, it would be the Men in White. Prison is a dark place. The lament psalms, I figured, would speak into that darkness.

So I started my first class out at the prison on the lament psalms. I began ticking through all the cries of abandonment, grief, and protest—all the psalms where accusations are hurled at God.

But something surprising happened. To this day, it remains one of the most profound and spiritually shattering experiences of my life. I've never been the same since.

I was speaking about the lament psalms, and the Men and White pushed back on me.

"We get it," they said, "prison sucks. We're aware. We know the darkness, the feeling of abandonment, the godforsakenness. That's our life. So we don't need more of that. What we need in here are songs of hope."

I was stunned. And speechless. Because at that time, I was in a spiritual hole. I didn't have a lot of sunshine in me. Lament psalms I could talk about, all day long. Doubt I could do, but songs of hope? I didn't think I could sing those.

But that's what the Men in White needed. So slowly over the weeks and months, I started to sing songs of hope and restoration. Monday after Monday, I kept coming back to visions like the one in

Ezekiel, the Valley of Dry Bones. God asks the prophet a profound question, "Can these dead things come back to life again?" That's the question the men in the prison were facing in the darkness: Is new life possible? Can anything be resurrected from the wreckage of my life? Can dead things come back to life again?

God's song of hope in Ezekiel answers yes, dead things can come back to life again. And as I've sung that song out at the prison, I've gotten swept up in its melody. Slowly, my dead faith came back to life again.

I didn't bring God out to the prison. God was already there, waiting for me, a stranger God than I could have imagined—a God who embraced me in the tattooed arms of prisoners.

The same thing happened to me at Freedom. For weeks I came and sat in the pews, waiting for Jesus to show up. And just like in the prison, I found Jesus in people like Mr. John, and in Josh, Kristi, Henry, Maria and Robert, and Judy.

And Miss Beth.

Because of all my spiritual struggles when I started going to Freedom, I had lost my capacity for praise and worship, so Freedom came as a bit of a culture shock. The worship and praise at Freedom is enthusiastic and passionate. Hands are raised, we dance in the aisles, prayer veils are waved, and praise flags lifted up. I was 100 percent a fish out of water.

And Miss Beth, she was at the center of it all.

Beth had lived a hard life. She'd battled years of addiction, been homeless, and had troubled and abusive histories with men. But a few years before I started attending Freedom, Beth had given her life to Jesus, and over time, she became a fixture at Freedom—and then more than a fixture: one of our leaders. By the time I showed up, Beth had taken charge of Freedom's kitchen, cooking, organizing, and directing our weekly meals. When I helped clean up after the meals, Beth told me what to do.

Considerable though it was, Beth's biggest influence on Freedom actually wasn't in the kitchen, it was in the sanctuary. During worship, we dance in the aisles, and Beth had a dance all her own. She didn't like drawing attention to herself, so she stood off in a corner during worship. And there she would open her hands and sway—a movement slow and graceful.

Beth's dance affected everyone at Freedom. That dance gave others permission to move in their own ways. And for my part, Beth's dancing opened my heart. After years in the spiritual desert, I learned from Miss Beth how to worship again.

When Beth danced, she was transformed. She

glowed. I've never seen anything else like it. When Beth danced alone with God, she was baptized with grace, and her dance was beautiful to watch. As I was struggling with my faith, I watched Miss Beth worship, and I could see the grace of God, real and present, wash over her. How could a person with such a difficult life experience so much peace and joy? And not just Beth, but the entire Freedom community. Whatever Miss Beth and the Freedom community had found in Jesus, I said to myself, I wanted it.

Freedom Fellowship and Beth's dance taught me how to pray and worship again. And it saved my faith.

Last year, Beth was diagnosed with cancer. When someone is poor and doesn't have access to regular medical checkups, a cancer diagnosis is usually late in the game. Soon after the diagnosis, Beth was moved to hospice.

Jana and I went to visit Beth in the ICU before they moved her to hospice. Joe and Becky, our community ministers, were there. Because of the pain and medication, Beth was only sporadically lucid. Jana held one of Beth's hands, and Becky held the other. I stroked Beth's bare foot.

Even in all that pain, Beth was still worried about our Freedom family, worried about if the meals were being taken care of. Becky and Jana assured Beth that people were helping out, though it would take ten people to replace one Beth.

There were lots of tears. At one point Becky began to softly sing "Blessed Assurance" over Beth, and we all joined in.

Blessed assurance, Jesus is mine.
O what a foretaste of glory divine.
Heir of salvation, purchase of God,
Born of His Spirit, washed in His blood.

This is my story, this is my song,
praising my Savior all the day long;
this is my story, this is my song,
praising my Savior all the day long.

It was the perfect song for Beth. *This is my story, this is my song, praising my Savior all the day long.* No lyrics better capture Beth's faith and life, the grace that found her and caused her to dance.

Before we left, I put my hand on Beth's forehead and prayed Psalm 91 over her.

For he will command his angels concerning you
    to guard you in all your ways;
they will lift you up in their hands,

so that you will not strike your foot against
a stone.

After I finished reading the psalm, I stroked Beth's hair. I said good-bye to a woman who had helped save my faith. "Beth," I said, "you are one of the most beautiful people I have ever met."

The following Friday, Beth fell into the arms of the angels.

I went looking for God at Freedom and out at the prison. Trusting in the words of Jesus, I went looking for God in strangers. And I found Jesus disguised in Mr. Albert and the Men in White, in Robert, Mr. John, and Miss Beth.

On the Day of Judgment, we are going to ask Jesus, "Lord, when did we ever see you?"

"I was everywhere," will be his answer. "I was everywhere in disguise."

2

THE CIRCLE OF OUR AFFECTIONS

When I talk to groups about hospitality, I like to ask them this question: "What's the very first thing you think when you arrive at a gathering?" People ponder this, and a variety of answers are shared. Eventually someone says, "Are my friends here?" And everyone nods in acknowledgment. Yes, that's the question we recognize that each of us, automatically and unconsciously, asks when we get to a meeting or a party. It's the question on our minds when we walk into church or as we scan the crowd on the sideline of our kid's soccer game.

Are my friends here?

"And that," I declare to my audience, "is the

number-one problem with extending hospitality, the number-one reason why we don't extend hospitality the way Jesus did."

HEART PROBLEMS

Before it is anything, hospitality is a matter of the heart. Hospitality doesn't begin with a new church ministry or a new policy from the government, as well-meaning as those things may be. Hospitality begins inside our hearts, with our affections, with the tenderness and kindness that we extend toward others, even toward strangers—especially toward strangers. Jesus comes to us in disguise. "Welcome the ignored and marginalized," says Jesus, "and you welcome me."

While that seems simple, this "will to embrace," as the theologian Miroslav Volf describes it, doesn't come easily, and the reason has to do with the question people ask when they walk into a crowd: "Are my friends here?" It's here, with that question, that the problems start.

The reason we don't welcome the God who comes to us in strangers, Jesus in disguise, is that our affections are crimped, pinched, and this narrowing of our affections isn't because we are wicked and depraved. You are not a bad person when you look first for your friends. It's normal and natural.

The problem with strangers is that they are *strange*—sometimes really strange. They might even be scary. At the very least, welcoming strangers can be awkward and uncomfortable, simply because they're different. And that difference tempts us to narrow our attention and affections to the smaller group of people with whom we feel comfortable. Our failure to welcome others as Jesus welcomed is rooted in the natural and automatic narrowing of our affections from the many to the few, from the strange to the similar.

Hospitality is often described as making room, creating a space of welcome and embrace to receive the God who comes to us in strangers. But before hospitality can make space in the world or around your table, it has to begin closer to home, with an inward, emotional revolution. Hospitality begins as an *affectional capacity*, cultivating the ability to make room in our hearts for others. Hospitality starts with the "will to embrace," the spontaneous and unconditional welcome we extend toward others.

Our social world is an emotional ecosystem. Feelings of warmth and attraction create clusters of friends, cliques of sameness where like is attracted to like. Feelings also separate us, creating the domain of strangers, the people we feel uncomfortable around or people we barely notice or recognize.

For example, as a part of an event I was speaking at, Jana and I were housed at a very fancy resort catering to a wealthy clientele. Jana noticed that the staff at the resort were super nice and welcoming. "We've been so impressed with how nice and friendly the staff are here," Jana shared with a woman attending the Christian conference. "Are they?" the woman asked. "I hadn't noticed."

You can't welcome people when you don't even notice them.

GOD MAKES ROOM FOR US

I said that the original story of hospitality in the Bible is in Genesis 18, the hospitality Abraham shows to the Lord who visits him as three strangers. But there is a story of hospitality in the Bible even before the meal Abraham serves God under the oaks of Mamre. This act of hospitality is found at the very start of Genesis, with the creation of the cosmos.

It has always been a puzzle to think about how God is everywhere. God is omnipresent, as we like to say. So where is Creation located in relation to God? Since God is everywhere, we can't be *outside* of God or *next to* God. So if we're not outside of God or next to God, it stands to reason that we are, somehow, *inside* of God.

There's a beautiful idea in the Jewish mystical tradition that expresses this notion that we exist on the inside of God. The idea is called *tzimtzum*. *Tzimtzum* is the Hebrew word for constriction or contraction. In the Jewish mystical tradition, *tzimtzum* is the belief that God constricted and withdrew God's self to make space for creation. *We exist because God makes room for us.* Creation is the hospitality of God.[1]

Importantly, God makes this space *within God's own self*. God makes room and welcomes creation within God's very own being.

In a similar way, hospitality is making room within ourselves. Primarily and most intimately, we make room within our hearts, mirroring the hospitality of God in making room for creation. And as God makes room for us in God's life, we welcome others into our homes and to our tables. We make room for each other because God made room for us. "Welcome one another," Paul says in Romans 15:7 (NRSV), "as Christ has welcomed you."

---

1. These ideas, the *tzimtzum* as the hospitality of God, come from Jürgen Moltmann. See Jürgen Moltmann, *The Trinity and the Kingdom: The Doctrine of God* (Minneapolis: Fortress Press, 1993).

THE TERRITORY OF OUR KINDNESS

The walls we have to tear down to make room for each other are rarely physical. The walls that separate us are mostly psychological. Feelings are what exclude people from our friendship and dinner table: ignoring versus noticing, suspicion versus trust, exclusion versus embrace.

To describe how our affections carve up the world into friends versus strangers, the ethicist Peter Singer uses an idea he calls "the moral circle."[2] A moral circle is created by a simple two-step process. First, we identify our tribe. We make a distinction between friends and strangers. We locate our family, friends, peeps, and BFFs. Everyone in this group is inside my moral circle. Everyone else is a stranger. So that's step one: make a distinction between friend and stranger, between insider and outsider.

The second step is this: extend kindness toward those on the inside of your moral circle. Consider the roots of the word *kindness*—kin and kind. Kindness is the feeling I extend toward my kin (my tribe, my people, my friends), toward those who are the same *kind* of people as me.

Our affections are for sameness—like attracted

---

2. Peter Singer, *The Expanding Circle: Ethics and Sociobiology* (New York: Farrar, Straus & Giroux, 1981).

to like, as Aristotle noticed millennia ago. We're drawn toward the similar and the familiar. We care and look out for "our kind."

There is goodness in this dynamic—our love for family and friends, our loyalty to our tribe and "our people"—but there is also much darkness. The moral circle highlights our natural tendency to restrict our kindness to the few rather than to the many, limiting our ability to see or notice the stranger, let alone welcome him or her. Because the walls that separate us begin with our emotions, only a few people are admitted into the circle of our affections, the circumference of our care.

And if all that sounds a little abstract, let's make it practical.

Consider how we treat servers at restaurants, a job I did during college. Much of the trauma I experienced in that job was doled out by the Sunday church crowd, since I worked Sunday lunches.

Imagine that your best friend gets a new job as a server at a restaurant, and tonight is her first night waiting tables. You and a group plan to surprise your friend by going to the restaurant. You arrive and ask to be seated in her section. You wait for your friend to come to the table for the big surprise.

When your friend arrives, she's surprised. She's touched and happy to see everyone. But this first night, she tells you, has been a night from hell. Her orders are coming out late or wrong. She's getting behind on taking care of her tables, and the customers are getting upset. She's "in the weeds," as they say in the restaurant industry. So when you see your friend in this situation, distressed and upset, what do you say to her?

Friends would say something like this: "Don't worry about us. Take care of the other tables first. We'll wait." It's the obvious answer. Of course that's how we'd treat a friend, because our friend is *inside* our moral circle. Naturally and automatically, our friend receives our kindness. That's how we treat people inside the circle of our affections.

Let's now imagine something similar but a bit different. Imagine a different night when you and your friends go out. While you're eating at the restaurant, you don't really notice it's a busy night. You also don't notice the signs of stress from your server—her perspiration and her hurry. You hardly look at her at all. All you notice is that the service isn't as quick as you'd like. So you get annoyed and upset. You stop making eye contact with the server. Maybe someone at the table makes a joke at her expense. And at the end of the night, you leave a small tip and perhaps a bad comment card so she can get yelled at by the manager.

Let's contrast these two examples. Two stressed-out and busy servers, treated so differently. And why? Because one server, our friend, is inside our moral circle, and that server gets our kindness.

But here's the deal. There is no great moral sacrifice on our part in showing kindness to a friend. We don't even think about it, it's so natural; it's just what we do for our friends. Kindness inside the circle of our affections is as natural as breathing.

But what about the other server, the one we don't know, who doesn't get kindness? She gets treated poorly because she's a stranger. She's outside our moral circle.

Here's the deal about that stranger. That server is somebody's friend. She's somebody's sister, somebody's daughter, somebody's mother, somebody's wife. That server is inside someone's moral circle. *Somebody* loves her—just not *us*.

This is why looking for our friends is the number-one problem we face in extending hospitality to strangers. When we look for and only notice our friends, the people like us, we reduce the territory of our kindness.

Hospitality is *expanding the moral circle* to make room in our hearts for each other.

The Early Church Expands the Moral Circle

Failing to make room isn't a modern problem. Ignoring people outside our moral circles has always been something Christians have struggled with. Consider the very first division in the early church. In Acts 6, a dispute breaks out among Jesus's followers. Here's what happened: "In those days when the number of disciples was increasing, the Hellenistic Jews among them complained against the Hebraic Jews because their widows were being overlooked in the daily distribution of food." (Acts 6:1). The Hellenistic Jews were Jews who had lived abroad among the Roman colonies and who spoke Greek. The Hebraic Jews were the Jews who spoke Hebrew and had lived their lives in Judea. The division in the church was ethnic prejudice, the Hebrews looking down their noses at the Hellenists. The Hebraic Jews felt that they were the *true* Jews because they were Judean natives and spoke Hebrew. The Hellenists were viewed with contempt for losing touch with their ethnic and religious roots. "Imagine calling yourself a Jew," we can hear the Hebrews disdainfully mutter, "when you can't even speak Hebrew!"

And so the moral circle collapsed, the circle of affections pinched. The widows of the Hellenists began to be ignored. An affectional barrier emerged, separating the two ethnic groups. You can see the whole dynamic playing out in Acts 6 just as it does in our communities: the Hebrews and Hellenists would show up to gatherings, and their first thought was, "Are my friends here?" That's how the division began.

As another example, consider the dispute between Peter and Paul recounted in Galatians 1. Peter had come to the church at Antioch, where many Gentiles were accepting Jesus. Peter, a Jew, began breaking bread with these Gentile converts. But when some Jewish Christians from the Jerusalem church visited, they convinced Peter to stop eating with the Gentile Christians. Once again, the moral circle collapsed; Jewish Christians only wanted to eat with other Jewish Christians and exclude their Gentile brothers and sisters. We can easily imagine a gathering of Antiochian Christians, the two groups scanning the crowd, sorting people into insiders and outsiders. These cliques outraged Paul, so he confronted Peter's failure of hospitality. According to Paul, when the moral circle collapses, the gospel is at stake.

Nothing has changed. Just like the early followers of Jesus, we're still carving up the world into insiders and outsiders, friends and strangers, people like me and people who aren't. We still have people living outside the circle of our affections. The divisions are no longer Jew versus Gentile or Hebrew versus Hellenist. Our divisions are more likely to be Republican versus Democrat, black versus white, rich versus poor, or citizen versus refugee.

Or even more simply: friends versus strangers.

These are the locations where we find our care, attention, and affections pinched and narrowed. A few we hold close to our hearts, and all the rest, even within the church, we hold at a distance.

Hospitality, expanding the moral circle, is how the early Christians overcame these ethnic and racial divisions. Because the gospel was at stake. In Acts 6, they began to care for those they were ignoring. In Galatians 1, the gospel demanded that Peter resume breaking bread with the people he was excluding. Hospitality is exactly how we'll overcome our own present-day divisions. We care for and break bread with those we ignore and exclude. But it starts with our hearts, with tearing down the emotional walls that keep from seeing the stranger God.

Hospitality begins with widening the circle of our affections, like treating that server refilling your water as a brother, sister and friend.

3

YES, AND

I'm convinced that every Christian should take lessons in improv comedy.

My wife, Jana, is a high school drama teacher, and her favorite thing to teach is improv. The number-one rule of improv is "Yes, and."

An improv scene starts when your partner begins by making you an "offer." For example, your partner runs to you and says in a terrified voice, "Quick, hide! They're coming!" That's her offer to you. The offer is a situational premise. Neither of you knows who or what you both are hiding from. Neither of you knows who is coming or why they're so scary—that's what will be discovered as you build upon the offer.

What you're supposed to do with the offer is accept it and add to it. What you're not supposed to do is reject or deny the offer; that's called *blocking*.

If your partner runs out and says, "Quick, hide! They're coming!" you shouldn't respond with "No they aren't" or "There's nobody there." That would be blocking the offer, rejecting the premise with a no.

So the first rule of improv is saying yes to the offer. You affirm the offer's truth and then add to it, handing another offer back to your partner. Your partner runs out and says, "Quick, hide! They're coming!" You duck behind a chair and say, "Oh, no, I knew they would find us!" By accepting the offer and ducking behind a chair, responding to the offer with a yes rather than a no, you give the scene forward momentum. We in the audience know something scary is coming, and two terrified people are rushing to hide. We lean in to see what will happen next.

The joy of improv is that your partner can make you a crazy, unexpected offer. If you've ever watched a great improv team, these offers electrify the audience because we know they're not going to be blocked; they'll be accepted with the yes, so we hang on the edge of our seats, eager to see where this crazy roller-coaster ride will go. That's the thrill of improv comedy: how accepting the offers of your partner take you both and your audience on an amazing adventure.

Christians can learn a lot from "Yes, and."[1] At its heart, hospitality is welcoming people with a yes instead of blocking them with a no.

ORDER IS EVERYTHING

In the first chapter of the Gospel of Mark, a leper comes to Jesus, falling at Jesus's feet. The mere fact that Jesus allowed the man to get to his feet was shocking. In the first century, people ran from lepers. According to the Jewish law, lepers had to live alone, separated from society, and had to yell, "Unclean! Unclean!" when they walked through the streets, giving everyone else a warning and time to back away (Leviticus 13:45–46). But Jesus stands his ground and allows the man to come very close. "If you are willing," the leper says, "you can make me clean."

"I am willing," Jesus says. And then Jesus does something even more shocking: he reaches out and touches the leper. You can almost hear the people gasp in disbelief.

---

1. In fact, in my book *Reviving Old Scratch* (Minneapolis: Fortress Press, 2016), I use "yes, and" to talk about how to read the Bible. In this book, I want to use "yes, and" to make a different point: how we should treat people.

Then, after touching the man, Jesus says, "Be clean!"

Notice how Jesus welcomes the leper with a yes instead of the expected, blocking no. Jesus's touch was his yes, his welcoming of the leper into the circle of his affections. I think that touch had more healing in it than the cleansing that followed, for lepers lived alone, and they spent their days watching people run away when they approached. When was the last time this man had been touched with any warmth or affection? I'm guessing that Jesus held that touch for a few long seconds.

Most importantly, Jesus touched the man *before* he cleansed him, while he was still unclean. And in the eyes of the law, by touching the leper, Jesus became unclean. Embrace came first, followed by cleansing, and we should ponder the significance of that ordering.

Miroslav Volf says that hospitality begins with "the will to embrace."[2] And just as in Mark 1, the will to embrace is all about the order. The will to embrace, according to Volf, is the affirmation of a person's worth, dignity, and humanity prior to any other judgments we make of the person. Jesus's touch is the perfect illustration of the will to

2. Miroslav Volf, *Exclusion and Embrace* (Nashville: Abingdon, 1996).

embrace. Jesus doesn't first see a leper, he sees a human being. Everyone else had the order backward. The crowd saw the leprosy first and then the man. Whereas Jesus's touch welcomed the man with an affirming yes, the crowd meets the leper with a blocking no.

The reason the church so often fails to welcome the lepers of our day and time is that we get the order of embrace all wrong. Consider if the order of the story had been reversed. It's a different story if Jesus yells, "Be clean!" from a distance and only then allows the healed man to approach. Yet that's exactly what the church does. Instead of touching lepers while they are lepers, as Jesus did, the church tells people to get cleaned up *before* they can be accepted and welcomed. "Clean up your act first," the church tells the world, "and then we'll embrace you."

Order is everything. We welcome people into the circle of our affections when we unconditionally embrace their humanity *before* we sort, judge, or evaluate them by any other criteria or standards. Where everyone else saw a leper, Jesus saw a human being. Affectionally, that ordering makes all the difference. Think of all the ways we judge each other, the ways we sort and label each other before we see and embrace each other as human beings. Before we see a woman or a Democrat or a lesbian or a home-less person or prisoner or minority or an addict or a Muslim, or any other label we can imagine, we must see the human being first. That's the will to embrace, the first step in the dance of hospitality.

This is a huge emotional challenge. When we see each other, in the world or on social media, we usually see the labels first: Democrat or Republican, male or female, white or black, gay or straight, Chris-tian or Muslim. And those labels trigger strong feel-ings in us, negative feelings that narrow the circle of our affections. Faster than the blink of an eye, before we even notice it, the will to embrace is lost. In our hearts, we've blocked each other with a no.

And once that happens, once I'm dealing with a "gay person" or a "Republican" or a "black person" or a "Muslim," rather than a human being with a name and a story, things quickly go downhill. We start to dehumanize and then demonize each other, all because we didn't secure the will to embrace at the very start. We didn't lead with a yes.

This is why the common advice "Love the sinner but hate the sin" is so ineffective. I was told in church when I was young that we can balance our commitments to both love and holiness by making a distinction between people and their behavior. We can love the people ("love the sinner") while hating their behavior ("hate the sin"). That seems like a neat and tidy bit of advice, but we've all seen how it fails in practice. When a group of Christians really hate a sin, they can't help growing angry at the people engaging in that sin. The distinction in "love sinners, hate sin" is ultimately impossible to maintain because it excludes the will to embrace. People are seen *first* as "sinners." That's the fatal mistake that happens right out of the gate, and it dooms the whole project. Order is everything. When we start by viewing people through their sins—or any other label—we lose track of their humanity. We've expelled them from the circle of our affections, and the process of dehumanization has already begun.

This is why social media has become so toxic. When we engage on social media, all we have are the labels. We see each other first on social media as liberal or conservative, as male or female, as white or black, as gay or straight, as Christian or Muslim. Because we can't look each other in the eye on social media, because we cannot touch each other the way Jesus touched the leper, the will to embrace is lost. And from there, again, it all goes downhill. You've seen how we treat each other on social media, so you know exactly what I'm talking about. And it's all because we don't secure the will to embrace at the start.

I've asked many audiences, "Do you think it's possible to both hate the sin and love the sinner?" People are generally split on the question. On the one hand, we've all witnessed or experienced Christians being hateful and judgmental. So half the people in my audiences express skepticism that this balance is possible, suspecting that hatred of sin inevitably leads to hatred of sinners. We've all seen the "God Hates Fags" signs carried by members of the Westboro Baptist Church.

But many people in my audiences say it is possible to both hate the sin and love the sinner. When I ask them to share personal examples of this, the answers are very revealing, and they illustrate the ordering of the will to embrace. The two most common examples I've heard about someone successfully loving the sinner while hating the sin sound like these:

"My brother is an addict. I hate what his addiction is doing to him. But I love my brother."

"Our daughter came out to us as gay. We don't agree with her lifestyle, but she's our daughter. So we love her unconditionally."

Notice something interesting in these responses. In both cases, the will to embrace came *before* the addiction and the coming out. And that embrace, that love, couldn't be severed, would never be severed, no matter what—because the will to embrace came first. Order, indeed, is everything.

Phrased differently, the reason love persists after the addiction or the coming out is because that brother, sister, or friend was *already inside* our moral circle, already embraced within the circle of our affections. This is what is missing when we try to love strangers and "sinners" abstractly and anonymously as we talk about each other on social media and in political debates. These strangers and "sinners" are outside our moral circles. Consequently, right at the start, we've already taken quite a few steps down the path of dehumanization and demonization. "God Hates Fags" and "Build That Wall!" signs are at the end of that road.

But those signs don't show up when we're talking about a son or daughter, sister or brother. The will to embrace holds them close, unconditionally so. Hospitality is extending this unconditional embrace to all of humanity, expanding the moral circle to treat everyone as family and friend.

Just as Jesus did.

Hospitality for Demons and Dragons

The author Peter Rollins has created a wonderful parable about the will to embrace; he titled it "Salvation for a Demon."[3] The parable is about a kindly old priest, known far and wide for his hospitality. Late one night, in the dead of winter, there was an ominous knock at the cathedral door. The priest hurried to open the door, concerned about a traveler being left out in the cold. Upon the opening the door, the gentle priest found a towering, terrifying demon.

Without hesitation, the kindly priest welcomed the demon into the church. As the priest finished with his evening devotions, the demon prowled the church, spewing curses and blasphemies.

When the priest retired to go home, the demon followed. Again, without hesitation, the priest welcomed the demon into his home and calmly prepared them both a meal. All the while, the demon cursed and mocked the priest.

Here's the climax of the parable:

The demon then ate the meal that was provided and afterward turned his attention to the priest,

3. Peter Rollins, *The Orthodox Heretic and Other Impossible Tales* (Brewster, MA: Paraclete, 2009), 26–27.

"Old man, you welcomed me first into your church and then into your house. I have one more request for you: will you now welcome me into your heart?"

"Why, of course," said the priest, "what I have is yours and what I am is yours."

This heartfelt response brought the demon to a standstill.... For the demon was unable to rob him of his kindness and his hospitality, his love and his compassion....

What happened to that demon after this meeting with the elderly priest is anyone's guess. Some say that although he left that place empty-handed he received more than he could ever have imagined.

And the priest? He simply ascended his stairs, got into bed and drifted off to sleep, all the time wondering what guise his Christ would take next.

This delightfully subversive parable is a profound illustration of both the ordering and the transformative power of the will to embrace. Demonization is overcome when we welcome each other into our hearts.

This parable of radical hospitality to "demons"

happens in real life. Consider the example of Daryl Davis, an African American musician who has spent his life sitting down and befriending Ku Klux Klan members. Dozens of former KKK members have left the Klan because Davis was willing to enter into conversation, relationship, and eventually friendship with them. As he recounts in the award-winning documentary *Accidental Courtesy*,[4] Davis's strategy in converting Klan members is simple: "You invite somebody to the table." That invitation to table embodies the order of the will to embrace, seeing a human being before the Klan hood, and the healing power of hospitality. Daryl Davis has the robes of former Grand Dragons of the KKK to prove it.

YES, *AND . . .*

Talking about hospitality to demons and white supremacists might have you wondering: Does the will to embrace mean we never talk about sin? Or does the will to embrace mean we never talk about truth and justice? Jesus does go on to cleanse the leper in Mark 1. And Jesus did say to the woman

4. *Accidental Courtesy: Daryl Davis, Race & America*, directed by Matt Ornstein (Sound & Vision, 2015); for more details, see the film's website, http://accidentalcourtesy.com.

caught in the act of adultery, "Go and sin no more." And yes, Jesus broke bread with tax collectors and sinners, but didn't the apostle Paul tell the church in Corinth to expel an immoral brother and not to eat with him?

The call to hospitality raises these questions about sin, truth, justice, and safety. Does hospitality have any limits or boundaries? Conservative Christians tend to worry about welcoming sinners, wondering if hospitality to sinners will cause us to go light on sin and dilute our moral witness to the world. Progressive Christians tend to worry about welcoming abusers and oppressors, fearing that hospitality will cause us to avoid hard and uncomfortable truths about privilege and injustice. Progressive Christians also worry that hospitality to abusers and oppressors will endanger the creation of safe spaces for victims.

I was once a co-presenter at a conference with Chris Haw, co-author of the best-selling book *Jesus for President*. During my session, I was advocating for open Communion as an expression of hospitality. Open Communion is a church practice where anyone and everyone is invited to participate in the Lord's Supper (also called Holy Communion or the Eucharist). As we like to say at my church before the Lord's Supper, "Everyone is welcome to the table."

After my talk about how open Communion is an act of hospitality, Chris asked me, "Would you allow torturers to partake of the Lord's Supper?"

The question comes from William Cavanaugh's book *Torture and Eucharist*.[5] In this book, Cavanaugh examines how the Catholic Church responded to the torture regime of the Chilean dictator Augusto Pinochet. Pinochet took power in a coup d'état in September 1973. After taking power, Pinochet intimidated, killed, and tortured rivals and those not supportive of his government. Many Chileans were "disappeared" arrested in the middle of the night and never heard from again.

Chile was a Catholic nation, so Pinochet's thugs went to Mass alongside the citizens they were torturing and the families of disappeared loved ones—the tortured and torturers coming forward together to partake of the Eucharist.

The Catholic Church found this to be an intolerable situation. So they excommunicated the torturers, refusing to let them take the Eucharist.

That was the background of Chris's question to me. Aren't some sins—like torture—so egregious they demand we expel people from our community? Aren't there limits to hospitality?

5. William T. Cavanaugh, *Torture and Eucharist: Theology, Politics, and the Body of Christ* (Malden, MA: Blackwell, 2010).

It's a difficult question, and opinions vary. It seems good and reasonable to deny the Eucharist to torturers. But I've shared Chris's question with advocates of open Communion, and they respond with a question of their own: Didn't Jesus *already* give his body and blood for torturers when he died on the cross for them? If so, who are we to put up a "Keep Out" sign around the body and blood of the Eucharist? Can we deny to others, even to torturers, what Christ has already freely given away?

These are thorny issues. I bring up the controversies about open Communion simply to illustrate that hospitality may have limits. At the very least, people of good will can disagree about where the limits, if any, might be.

But I think we can find some solid common ground if we go back to our improv lesson. Remember, the rule is "yes, *and.*" We lead with embrace, unconditionally accepting the humanity of all—sinner and saint, oppressor and oppressed. But the *yes* is followed by an *and.* Conversations and decisions about holiness, truth telling, justice, and boundaries follow the will to embrace.

But here's the critical part that cannot be missed: these conversations have to follow the will to embrace if they are to be humane, full of justice and mercy, truth and grace. If the will to embrace is not secured, any conversation about holiness becomes harsh, abusive, and judgmental, the exact opposite of how we see Jesus treat sinners in the Gospels. Similarly, if the will to embrace is not secured in the pursuit of truth and justice, we are tempted to hate oppressors, failing to love our enemies as Jesus commanded.

The will to embrace doesn't eclipse conversations about sin and oppression. Instead, it prioritizes everyone's humanity as holiness and justice are being pursued. It is the will to embrace—*yes*, followed by *and*—that keeps us from dehumanizing and demonizing each other when conversations and decisions about holiness and justice get difficult.

Order is everything. The will to embrace comes first, everything else follows. Yes, and.

So let that be our prayer.

May we all learn to improv well.

PART II

THE EMOTIONAL BATTLEFIELD

4

HITLER'S SWEATER AND COOTIES FOR GROWN-UPS

Do you remember playing cooties on the playground as a child? "Cooties" are those imaginary germs that children use to play infection games. When I was a child, girls had cooties, so you never wanted to go near or touch a girl. The girls, of course, disputed this. According to the girls, it was the boys who had cooties, so they avoided us. Our arguments on the playground often focused on finding the true source of our epidemics: Who *really* had the cooties—the boys or the girls? Our playground talk sounded like CDC specialists tracking down an Ebola outbreak.

We don't outgrow this game. Adults play cooties as well. Think of all the adjectives we use to convey feelings of revulsion about people we don't like. We call people creepy, slimy, sleazy, icky, rotten, repellant, lousy, detestable, offensive, nasty, awful, bad, distasteful, loathsome, horrible, vile, vulgar, trash, obnoxious, repugnant, gross, stinking, nauseating, revolting, and beastly. Each of these adjectives points to emotions of interpersonal revulsion. As grown-ups, we don't think people have actual cooties, but the social emotions associated with cooties stick with us and cause us to avoid each other, using behavior not unlike that of our childhood playgrounds. These feelings of revulsion or contempt are the feelings of social avoidance and exclusion, the emotions that narrow the circle of our affections. These feelings are the battleground of hospitality.

WOULD YOU TRY ON HITLER'S SWEATER?

Truth be told, it's more than feelings. Even as adults we behave as if we still believe in cooties. For example, psychologists have brought people into a laboratory to show them an old sweater.[1] They tell the participants that the sweater was once owned and worn by Adolf Hitler, and they invite the subjects to put the sweater on. Would they be willing to do that? And if they did, how would it make them feel, wearing Hitler's sweater?

Most people refuse to put the sweater on. Those who do put it on feel icky and uncomfortable wearing it.

True, we don't believe in actual cooties, but we act as if we think Hitler's sweater has been contaminated by his evil. We don't want to wear or be near Hitler's sweater because we feel that it's somehow morally polluted, and we're worried about that evil rubbing off on us.

We know this is an irrational response. Evil isn't a germ that can contaminate fabric, yet we treat the sweater as if it has a moral virus. It's totally illogical, but that's how we treat moral failings.[2] Psychologically, we treat sin as if it were cooties, a moral contaminant that is passed via physical contact, which becomes another source of interpersonal revulsion. If we emotionally treat sin as if it were cooties, we

1. C. Nemeroff and P. Rozin, "The Contagion Concept in Adult Thinking in the United States: Transmission of Germs and Interpersonal Influence," *Ethos* 22 (1994): 158–86.
2. Psychologists call this irrationality "magical thinking." See Paul Rozin et al., "Operation of the Laws of Sympathetic Magic in Disgust and Other Domains," *Journal of Personality and Social Psychology* 50 (1986): 703–12.

naturally keep our distance from sinners. It doesn't make rational sense, but it's where our emotions lead us if we don't check them. These are the emotions that scandalized the Pharisees and religious leaders about Jesus's behavior in the Gospels. "Why does your teacher eat with tax collectors and sinners?" they asked. When you experience sinners as a source of moral cooties, Jesus's hospitality to them is disturbing. What Jesus was doing didn't feel right.

This hasn't changed in the last 2,000 years. The psychology of moral cooties gives us another explanation about why the advice to "love the sinner, hate the sin" doesn't work so well. It's like Hitler's sweater. When we experience sin as a form of moral contamination, we can't help feeling emotionally uncomfortable around "sinners." We fear the sin will rub off on us, so we act like the Pharisees in the Gospels.

Consider another feature of contamination psychology called "negativity dominance."[3] Imagine I take an apple and a piece of dog poop, and I touch them together. I then offer you the apple. Would you

---

3. Carol Nemeroff and Paul Rozin, "The Makings of the Magical Mind," in *Imagining the Impossible: Magical, Scientific, and Religious Thinking in Children*, ed. Karl S. Rosengren, Carl N. Johnson, and Paul L. Harris (New York: Cambridge University Press, 2000), 1–34.

eat it? Of course not. The apple has been contaminated, ruined by its contact with the poop.

So it should work the other way, too: if the poop ruined the apple, then the apple should have made the poop delicious. But no, contamination doesn't work that way. It's not a two-way street. The poop ruins the apple, and the apple does nothing to the poop.

When it comes to contamination, the negative dominates the positive. That's negativity dominance. When the pure and the polluted come into contact, the pollutant wins. The pure becomes impure, but the pure does not purify the polluted. The poop always trumps the apple.

Now, in the world of food, this makes perfect sense. But notice what happens when we start treating people as if they were polluted substances. The Pharisees use this same reasoning about Jesus eating with tax collectors and sinners. When Jesus —the apple—and the sinners—the poop—make contact, who gets contaminated? Jesus does. Because that's how contamination works. That's negativity dominance.

When the Pharisees see the pure and the impure come into contact, the conclusion they draw—that Jesus is made unclean by eating with sinners—is natural and reasonable. That judgment feels right, because that's how contamination works. If we were standing there with the Pharisees, we'd make the exact same emotional judgment.

The point of all this is simply to highlight how hospitality is an emotional battleground. What Jesus was doing in the Gospels in welcoming tax collectors, sinners, and prostitutes felt strange; for those who saw him do it, it was emotionally counterintuitive and hard to compute. To practice hospitality, then, we are going to have to do some hard emotional work to overcome the feelings that cause us to avoid and exclude people. In a world of moral cooties, hospitality doesn't come very naturally to us. Hospitality demands emotional discipline and intentionality.

HOW ABOUT DRINKING SPIT OUT OF A DIXIE CUP?

I keep coming back to the phrase "the circle of our affections," because this is the case when it comes to these emotions of social revulsion and disgust. Consider the Dixie cup demonstration: How do you feel about swallowing the saliva in your mouth right now? No problem, right? Okay, how would you feel if I asked you to spit into a Dixie cup and then quickly drink it? That's a bit more disgusting, right?

But what's the actual physical difference between swallowing the spit in your mouth or spitting it out and quickly drinking it? There's not much physical difference, but there's a huge emotional difference. Swallowing the saliva in your mouth is no problem, but drinking the spit from a Dixie cup is disgusting.

What the Dixie cup demonstration illustrates is this: disgust is a boundary psychology.[4] I don't mind swallowing the saliva in my mouth because it's on the *inside* of me, a part of me. But once that saliva crosses the boundary of the body, once it's *outside* of me, it's no longer a part of me. And because it's no longer a part of me, feelings of revulsion rise up, and I push the Dixie cup away.

A circle of affections is at work here. An emotional boundary is erected between the inside and the outside, and feelings of revulsion and disgust act as border guards. That which is inside is treated kindly, as a part of me. But that which is outside, that which is not a part of me, is rejected with a feeling of disgust.

Ponder again the adjectives we use to evoke emotions of disgust toward people: creepy, gross, icky,

4. To read more about the Dixie cup experiment and boundary psychology, see my book *Unclean: Meditations on Purity, Hospitality, and Mortality* (Eugene, OR: Cascade, 2011).

revolting, slimy, rotten, nauseating, trashy, sleazy, or nasty. We're back in the world of cooties. These associations elicit feelings of revulsion, causing us to treat people like spit. We use these adjectives to associate people with filth and pollution, making it easier to exclude and, in extreme cases, exterminate them. Disgust triggers dehumanization.

The Dixie cup illustration shows us exactly how our emotions carve up the world into insiders and outsiders. This is how our emotions tell us . . .

> . . . who is inside our moral circle and who is outside
> . . . who gets treated with kindness and affection and who gets ignored or shoved away
> . . . who gets welcomed as a friend and who gets excluded as a stranger

When we treat people with disdain, revulsion, or contempt, we are expelling them from the circle of our affections. Emotionally, as in the Dixie cup experiment, we are treating these people as something alien, strange, and vile.

EMBRACING EUNUCHS

It's fascinating to observe how the church in the

book of Acts overcomes the social emotions of disgust and contamination to widen their moral circle. Prior to his ascension into heaven, Jesus commissioned his disciples to take good news of the kingdom into all the world, to those strange foreign people with weird accents. But the emotions of moral and social cooties interfered. The church was becoming an insular community of the same and similar.

We know that an emotional boundary associated with moral cooties was the problem because of how God challenges the church to expand the moral circle. The story is found in Acts 10. Peter is praying alone on a rooftop. There he sees a vision of unclean animals—animals the purity codes of Leviticus prohibited Jews from eating. And yet a voice from heaven commands, "Get up, Peter! Kill and eat." As a good Jew, Peter responds, "Surely not, Lord! I have never eaten anything impure or unclean." In response, the voice from heaven says, "Do not call anything impure that God has made clean." This happens three times, and three times the voice says, "Do not call anything impure that God has made clean."

The vision is all about disgust and contamination, but as the story unfolds, we come to see that the issue isn't really about unclean *food*. The issue facing the church was its rejection of unclean *people*. God uses the vision to explode the Dixie cup psychology of the church—how the church was excluding unclean people, treating them like spit. Feelings of social revulsion were crippling the mission of the church. So on that rooftop, God forces the church to overcome its fear of moral cooties to start acting like Jesus.

Another example of how the unclean were embraced within the moral circle of the church is found in in Acts 8, when Philip encounters the Ethiopian eunuch. The backstory goes back, once again, to the Levitical purity code, the same code that Jesus violated by touching lepers. Similar to the lepers, eunuchs were also unclean. As it says in Deuteronomy 23:1, "No one who has been emasculated by crushing or cutting may enter the assembly of the Lord." Since eunuchs lacked genitalia, they were strange and foreign, neither male nor female. Under the purity codes, this made eunuchs unclean. So the contamination logic of negativity dominance was enforced: eunuchs were excluded.

But the story doesn't end there. The Hebrew prophets had a way of pushing back on the purity codes. Jesus liked to quote the prophets to critique the purity concerns of the Pharisees. In Matthew 9, the Pharisees were scandalized by Jesus breaking bread with notorious sinners. So Jesus quoted the prophets, a line from Hosea 6:6. "Go and learn what this means. 'I desire mercy, not sacrifice.'" Mercy trumps your worries about purity.

In a similar way, the prophet Isaiah pushes back on the Levitical exclusion of eunuchs from the people of God. One day, declares Isaiah, the unclean eunuchs will be welcomed into the moral circle of the kingdom:

> Let no foreigner who is bound to the LORD say,
> "The LORD will surely exclude me from his
> people."
> And let no eunuch complain,
> "I am only a dry tree."
>
> For this is what the LORD says:
>
> "To the eunuchs who keep my Sabbaths,
> who choose what pleases me
> and hold fast to my covenant—
> to them I will give within my temple and its walls
> a memorial and a name
> better than sons and daughters;
> I will give them an everlasting name
> that will endure forever." (Isaiah 56:3–5)

The people the Levitical code excluded as unclean would be welcomed in. So we're not surprised in Acts 8 when Philip encounters a eunuch. This is no accidental meeting! The Holy Spirit placed Philip at this location specifically to embrace a eunuch—who is a foreigner with a strange African accent to boot. Here, at long last, is the fulfillment of Isaiah's prophecy! This is the eagerly awaited and hoped-for inclusion of the unclean, the will to embrace extended to the excluded and marginalized.

KISSING LEPERS

There's a famous story about Saint Francis of Assisi and a leper he meets on the road. From his earliest childhood, Francis had been mortally terrified of and disgusted by lepers. He fled at the sight of them and at the sound of the tinkling bells they wore to warn people of their approach.

One day, shortly after his conversion, Francis was walking down a road, when he saw a leper approaching.[5] Instinctively, Francis turned to flee, as he always did. But this time, Francis stopped. Overcome by a divine prompting, Francis turned back. He rushed toward the leper, embraced and kissed him.

5. Some versions of the story have Francis riding down the road.

From that day onward, Francis began to care for lepers—washing, feeding, and nursing them, often in appalling conditions. Leper colonies in the Middle Ages were foul, putrid places. But the lepers who had previously filled Francis with revulsion and disgust were now embraced as beloved brothers and sisters. Francis's moral circle had expanded, and revulsion was replaced with kindness. Others followed Francis's example. The early Franciscans became noteworthy for their ministry in leper colonies.

It's time for Christians to stop playing cooties and start following the examples of Francis and the early church. Feelings of revulsion and disgust collapse our moral circles. True, we might not run away from people the way Francis did. We're more likely to stand off to the side, wagging fingers of judgment, just as the Pharisees grumbled and fretted about Jesus. But this will take some work. It was emotionally difficult for Francis to turn around that day on the road, to move toward the leper against the churning tide of his disgust and fear, just as there was something strange and uncomfortable about Jesus hanging out with sinners and prostitutes. It didn't *feel* right. The first step toward hospitality rarely does. But that's how we begin to welcome the stranger God.

There's one last bit to the story about Francis

and the leper. After parting with the leper, Francis turned back to bid the man farewell. But when Francis turned around, he found himself all alone on the empty road. The leper had disappeared.

Jesus, once again, in disguise.

5

OUR DIRTY
LITTLE SECRET

"It looked deathless."

I was visiting a successful megachurch, to do some teaching for their hospitality and welcoming ministries. During my visit, I attended one of their worship services. The service was excellent—of high quality and well produced. I don't say that with any judgment; I enjoyed the worship very much.

The next morning, the staff members asked for some feedback about the worship service, especially any critical feedback I might have.

I thought for a moment and then said, "Well, the whole thing looked deathless."

They looked at me with puzzled expressions, so I elaborated. "The service was very well done," I said. "I loved it. But from start to finish, all I saw onstage were young, attractive, talented, fashionable, and hip people. I never saw anyone with white hair or in a wheelchair, or anyone with a disability. It was all bright, shiny, happy people, like a magazine or a TV show—no sign of death, decay, deformity, disability, dysfunction, or dementia."

My assessment is not all that surprising. Our churches tend to reflect what we value as Americans: youthfulness, energy, success. We don't like being reminded of failures of body or mind, or of failed dreams and aspirations. As children of the American dream, we applaud talent, success, youth, and beauty. So our worship stages rarely spotlight the elderly, the disabled, the sick, unemployed, weak, dying, or poor.

THE PORNOGRAPHY OF DEATH

Disgust is diverse. There are three kinds of disgust.[1] Core disgust is the heart of disgust, and it's focused on food—the revulsion we feel if we find a hair in our soup. Second, moral cooties, the discomfort we feel watching Jesus break bread with sinners, is called sociomoral disgust.

1. P. Rozin, J. Haidt, and C. R. McCauley, "Disgust," in *Handbook of Emotions*, 2nd ed., ed. M. Lewis & J. M. Haviland-Jones (New York: Guilford, 2000), 637–53.

The third kind of disgust, among North Americans especially, involves feelings of revulsion to the following things:

- Body fluids
- Gore
- Deformity
- Corpses
- Poor hygiene
- Animals

This list doesn't have a whole lot to do with food or morality, but there is a common thread. Can you see it?

The third type of disgust is called "animal reminder" or "mortality reminder" disgust. I think a better label is "body reminder" disgust, because the thread that ties the list together is that we can experience disgust and revulsion when we encounter things that remind us of the needs and vulnerabilities of the human body, a body subject to the forces of decay and death. We feel disgusted by the fragility and failures of the body, because it reminds us that we aren't gods or angels. The smells, fluids, and deformities of the body remind us that we are needy, dependent creatures.

As Americans who pride ourselves on success

and self-sufficiency, we're nauseated by neediness and dependency. Worse, we moralize it. We heap moral cooties upon the needy: not only is it shameful, but you're a bad person if you are poor.

Disgust gets associated with our bodies because disgust is an emotion that helps us push away any reminders that we will die one day. Disgust helps us pretend we're immortal. We like our world to look deathless, just like that worship stage at the church. We don't want to be reminded of human need and vulnerability. The body is a scandal.

American culture is characterized by "the denial of death," an avoidance to see, think, or talk about death.[2] This has been described as "the pornography of death."[3] Death is an illicit topic. You're morbid for talking about death in polite conversation. In the fantasyland that is the American dream—where bright, shiny people smile at us with perfect teeth from screens, magazine covers, and worship stages—death is our dirty little secret.

The problem with this fairy-tale world is that it is radically inhospitable to people who remind us of our physical needs and vulnerabilities—the elderly,

2. Ernest Becker, *The Denial of Death* (New York: Simon & Schuster, 1973).
3. Geoffrey Gorer, *Death, Grief, and Mourning* (Garden City, NY: Anchor, 1967).

the intellectually disabled, the physically disabled, the mentally ill, the homeless, the sick, the dying. In a world where need and dependency are pornographic, these people are pushed off the stages of the world or never invited up in the first place. They are banished from America's moral circle. We hide these people in homes, hospitals, and institutions. We ignore them as they sleep on the street.

They suffer so we can keep our dirty little secret.

SHAMING THE BODY

This isn't a modern problem. The early Christians shamed neediness as well. Consider James's admonition to some of the early followers of Jesus:

My brothers and sisters, believers in our glorious Lord Jesus Christ must not show favoritism. Suppose a man comes into your meeting wearing a gold ring and fine clothes, and a poor man in filthy old clothes also comes in. If you show special attention to the man wearing fine clothes and say, "Here's a good seat for you," but say to the poor man, "You stand there" or "Sit on the floor by my feet," have you not discriminated among yourselves and become judges with evil thoughts?

Listen, my dear brothers and sisters: Has not God chosen those who are poor in the eyes of the world to be rich in faith and to inherit the kingdom he promised those who love him? But you have dishonored the poor. (James 2:1–6a)

Just like us, the early Christians exalted the winners and shamed the failures. This schism between the winners and the losers, between the honored and the shamed, was one of the deepest divisions that ran through the early Christian communities. It's the same reason we don't like losers and failures on our worship stages.

Consider also Paul's admonition in 1 Corinthians 12, a text we often misinterpret. We're familiar with Paul's famous body metaphor in 1 Corinthians 12—how the community of believers, the body of Christ, is made up of different members, each with special spiritual talents and gifts. Some of us are eyes, some of us are hands, and some of us are feet. We often treat Paul's body metaphor as if it were a personality test. "What part of the body of Christ am I?" we ask. "What are my special talents and gifts?" But that's not the point of Paul's metaphor, that there are different gifts in the body. The point is that different gifts, different groups within the church, were being honored and shamed. Just as in the epistle of James, the wealthier members of the church in Corinth were shaming the poorer members. The wealthy patrons of the congregation were contemptuous of those who were servants and slaves.

So Paul steps in and tells the church to stop it. Here's how he begins: "The eye cannot say to the hand, 'I don't need you!' And the head cannot say to the feet, 'I don't need you!'" (1 Corinthians 12:21). The problem here isn't the diversity within the church, but that the rich members of the church were saying to the needier members, "I don't need you. You are unnecessary, unwanted, and unimportant." The wealthy members were treating people as discardable and disposable—as *trash*. We're back to those dehumanizing emotions. But in this case, the emotions weren't being triggered by moral cooties. This disgust was triggered by social class. The church was shaming the poor.

So Paul takes dead aim, calling out the shaming and arguing that "less honorable" and "unpresentable" people should not be treated with scorn but given "special honor." This *rehabilitative honoring*—giving honor, care, and attention to people who don't usually get our honor, care, and attention—allows the church to show "equal concern" for everyone:

Those parts of the body that seem to be weaker are indispensable, and the parts that we think are less honorable we treat with special honor. And the parts that are unpresentable are treated with special modesty, while our presentable parts need no special treatment. But God has put the body together, giving greater honor to the parts that lacked it, so that there should be no division in the body, but that its parts should have equal concern for each other. (1 Corinthians 12:22–25)

Hospitality doesn't shove unpresentable people into the corner. Hospitality welcomes them onto the stage and into the spotlight.

Hospitality extends special care and honor to people the American dream would rather hide. I remember a few years ago reading about the "The Great Shopping Cart War" between the Catholic Workers and the city of Los Angeles. The Catholic Worker movement, started by the Catholic activist Dorothy Day, is known for extending hospitality to the poor and homeless. Many of the homeless friends of the LA Catholic Workers lived on Skid Row. Lacking permanent housing, the residents of Skid Row kept their belongings in shopping carts. But people started complaining. The shopping carts were an eyesore. The highly visible shopping carts drew too much attention to the number of homeless people living on the streets of LA. Those shopping carts were a scandal to the deathless illusion of the American dream. So the police started confiscating the shopping carts, saying they were stolen property.

Seeing the belongings of their friends thrown onto the street, the LA Catholic Workers responded. They purchased shopping carts for their friends on Skid Row and gave them as gifts. A legal battle ensued between the city and the Workers. The Workers won. Apparently, it's not illegal in America to buy a friend a shopping cart.

I remember when I first met Kristi at the back of our church. Kristi is blind and unsteady on her feet, so she uses a wheelchair. When we first met, our church's auditorium wasn't wheelchair accessible. That, in itself, was an institutional hospitality problem. So when the church van driver brought Kristi into the auditorium, he put her along the back wall. Since there were no other seats along the back wall, Kristi sat there alone.

One day I asked her if she liked sitting in the back of the church along the wall. "Not really," she said. "Sometimes people step on my feet when they pass by."

That answer made me wince—hospitality failures all around. We weren't doing a very good job of showing Kristi "special honor" by putting her in the back, all alone, where people stepped on her feet.

In light of Paul's admonition 1 Corinthians 12, how can a community show someone like Kristi special and greater honor? For Kristi and me, it meant working with Dickie, the staff member in charge of the building, to identify and reserve a row in our auditorium where a wheelchair could safely fit, so that Kristi could sit with my family every Sunday. And that's how our friendship started.

WHEN IT'S YOUR SHEEP IN THE DITCH

We're calloused toward neediness and failure, because we're blinded to our own need and vulnerability. We lack empathy for people who lack health insurance, until we find ourselves without health insurance. We judge the unemployed, until we find ourselves looking for a job. We judge the divorced, right up to the point when we file for our own. We judge the addicted, until we find ourselves checking into the rehab center.

The will to embrace flows out of empathy and compassion. And compassion flows out of a recognition of our own weakness, vulnerability, and neediness.

In Matthew 12, Jesus's disciples were hungry. So they picked some grain in the fields to eat. Trouble was, it was the Sabbath day. So the Pharisees wagged their fingers: "Jesus, why are your followers breaking the Sabbath?"

Right after, Jesus enters a synagogue, where he finds a man with a physical deformity, a withered hand. But again, it was the Sabbath. So the Pharisees wait to see if Jesus will violate the Sabbath to perform a healing. Jesus gets angry at the onlookers and then asks a very interesting question: "How many of you, if your sheep fell into a ditch on the Sabbath, wouldn't pull it out?"

The point of Jesus's question is economic. Sheep weren't pets. Sheep meant dollar signs. The Pharisees would go after the sheep, even on the Sabbath, because their incomes were being affected. A modern spin on Jesus's question would be this: "How many of you, if you dropped your wallet on the sidewalk on the Sabbath, wouldn't pick it up?"

Jesus is making a point about need and empathy. The Pharisees judge the men in the grain field because the Pharisees are well fed. The Pharisees don't see the need of the man with the deformity because they are whole and providing for their families. The Pharisees lack empathy because their momentary self-sufficiency has blinded them to their own need and vulnerability. So Jesus points it out to them: "You lack compassion for this man's need because you cannot see your own need."

It's no surprise that the issues in Matthew 12 highlight the needs and vulnerabilities of the body—hunger and physical deformity. These are the same disgust triggers we've been talking about. Just like the Pharisees, we lack empathy for the needs of others because we don't admit and embrace our own vulnerability. It's easy to judge the needs of others until we find ourselves needing a doctor, a job, a car, or a few bucks to pay the rent. We're calloused because we think we're immune to loss and failure. But Jesus reminds us of our dirty little secret. We're all needy. We're all vulnerable. So be kind and compassionate—because one day, it's going to be your sheep that falls into the ditch.

THE SEVENTH WORK OF MERCY

In Matthew 25, Jesus appears incognito to the sheep and goats in six encounters: feeding the hungry, giving water to the thirsty, clothing the naked, giving shelter to the homeless, visiting the prisoner, and visiting the sick. In the Catholic tradition, these activities are collectively called "the works of mercy." But they also include a seventh work that's not mentioned in Matthew 25: burying the dead.

This seventh work of mercy comes from the Old Testament book of Tobit, a book found in Catholic but not in Protestant Bibles. Tobit is the story of Tobit, a faithful Israelite living in Nineveh, where he'd been deported after the Assyrian conquest of Israel. Tobit cares for his fellow refugees, feeding the hungry and clothing the naked, but he takes special pains to bury fellow Jews killed by the Assyrian king. Refusing to let his countrymen rot out in the open air, at night Tobit collected and buried the dead. Because of Tobit's story, during the Middle Ages burying the dead was added to the list in Matthew 25 as the seventh work of mercy.

A couple of years ago, I was speaking at the same conference as Danny Cortez, pastor of New Life Community church in California. One morning, Jana and I were able to have breakfast with Danny and his wife, Abby. We spent most of our time talking about the crazy year Danny had experienced.

Danny had been in the eye of a social-media hurricane. Danny was an evangelical pastor, but he'd been reconsidering his views about LGBT persons, eventually reaching a more welcoming and inclusive position. Right after he'd changed his views, Danny's son came out to him as gay. The timing of Danny's theological shift with his son's coming out couldn't have been any better, or worse, depending upon where you stood in the culture wars.

Controversy ensued. Danny's sermon sharing his story, "Why I Changed My Mind on Homosexuality," was posted on YouTube, where it became the focus of furious debate. Among progressive Christians, Danny was a hero. Among evangelicals, Danny was a turncoat and heretic.

The Internet notoriety took its toll. Being batted around like a ball in the culture wars, with hundreds of people simultaneously lauding or vilifying you, was hard on Danny and his family.

So I asked Danny, "What has given you life over the past year? Where have you been able to feel close to God?"

Danny's answer surprised me. During the year when Danny was a social-media celebrity, he had begun working as a chaplain for an organization that provided hospice care for the homeless. As the social-media storms raged, Danny's phone would ring, and he would be beckoned to the bedside of a homeless person in his or her final days and moments. There was no one else to call. These homeless men and women were alone in the world—no family, no friends. But they wouldn't die alone. Danny would be there.

Those moments were holy and sacred for Danny. I asked Danny what was so powerful about the experience. "There's nothing I can do to fix it," said Danny, "All I can do is be present." In the face of his own impotence and limitations, the essence of our shared humanity was revealed. What we crave most in life is companionship—to have someone there, holding our hand, bearing witness to our life. That was the gift Danny gave and received.

Sitting by a dying homeless person is about as far from the American dream as you can get. That is the very bottom rung of the ladder. And that's where Danny found God: in the seventh work of mercy.

In this deathless fantasyland, full of bright, shiny people with tans and perfect teeth, Jesus comes to us in the strangest and most unlikely of places. Jesus comes to us in the failures—in the discarded, the jobless, and the addicted. Jesus comes to us in the crazed and demented, in the deformed and disabled.

Jesus comes to us in a wheelchair or pushing a cart on Skid Row.

6

THE MURDERER
IN OUR HEART

I think dark thoughts. I'm not murderous, but in the face of human ignorance and stupidity, my mind turns venomous.

And that's just when I'm standing in line at the grocery store.

Social media and cable news make it worse. The idiocy, hypocrisy, and insanity of it all fill me with rage.

"People are idiots!" I mutter to myself. I've muttered this out loud so many times that my family thinks it's my life's motto. "Hey Dad," my son will say, "You know how you're always saying 'People are idiots'? Well, guess what happened at school today. . . ."

Ouch. I need to start biting my tongue at home.

THE MOST TOXIC EMOTION

John Gottman, a leading expert on marriage, has done research on how emotions in marital spats predict subsequent divorce. His research has found that one emotion is especially toxic.[1] If you see this emotion a great deal in marital arguments, there's a good chance the couple is headed for trouble. Can you guess what emotion it is?

You might think it would be anger. It's not. While anger can be strong and hot, anger isn't a dehumanizing emotion. You can be angry at someone while holding onto the will to embrace. Occasional anger doesn't undermine love.

The most toxic emotion in a marriage is contempt. Contempt is the emotion most predictive of divorce.

The reason for this is that contempt, like disgust, is a dehumanizing emotion. Contempt is the sibling of disgust. Psychologists have noted that both emotions involve a wrinkling of the nose, suggesting that both emotions are rooted in a food-evaluation system, smelling food to make sure it's not contaminated or rotten. When we feel disgust, even at

---

1. Sybil Carrère and John M. Gottman, "Predicting Divorce among Newlyweds from the First Three Minutes of a Marital Conflict Discussion," *Family Process* 38 (1999): 293–301.

people, we wrinkle our noses, as if the person we dislike were a piece of rotten meat. In a similar way, emotions of contempt, disdain, and scorn involve sniffing and turning up our noses at people. Snobs are portrayed with their noses in the air, as if the lowlifes beneath them stink.

Contempt is a type of disgust, but different in two ways. First, beyond a feeling of revulsion, contempt has an angry edge to it. This is the anger that causes me to mutter "People are idiots!" when I'm watching social media and cable TV. Second, contempt is hierarchical in nature. The revulsion is directed downward, toward the people beneath us. The haughty and elite look *down* on people. Contempt is a feeling of superiority, often moral superiority.

This is why contempt is so toxic in a marriage. Anger is an egalitarian emotion. You can be angry with your spouse, but that doesn't mean you think your spouse is beneath you. Contempt implies that your spouse is inferior. And that's a problem.

And not just for a marriage. Contempt is toxic for any relationship. I might not feel disgust or revulsion around people, but whenever I mutter, "People are idiots," I'm dehumanizing them. Contempt marks others as less than human, less like ourselves—less smart, less moral, less worthy, or less important. This is why Jesus says calling people idiots is a form of killing. Contempt is affectional murder, a death in the heart.

You might not struggle with moral cooties, but everyone struggles with feelings of scorn and superiority. Think about all the disdain you feel looking through your social-media feed. A person might not be icky or disgusting, but the person can be an idiot or a jerk.

How do you feel about liberals or conservatives, Republicans or Democrats? Everywhere we turn, people are getting in our way, making stupid decisions, voting for the wrong candidates, and doing other things we find offensive. It's here, in these emotional trenches, where the battle to welcome God in strangers is either won or lost.

Hospitality isn't just about welcoming sinners; it's also about welcoming people we think are idiots. The will to embrace rescues people from the murderer in our hearts.

BREAKING DOWN THE WALL OF HOSTILITY

We don't deserve God's grace. Christ died for us while we were sinners. The worthy gave his life for the unworthy.

That's the message of grace many of us grew up with and still believe. Grace is a gift given to people who don't deserve it. That's what makes it grace.

That idea—it's grace because we don't deserve it—is so natural and widespread that we don't appreciate how strange and revolutionary it is. That's the argument John Barclay makes in his book *Paul and the Gift*.[2] Barclay points out that for most of human history, gifts—grace is just another word for gift—were supposed to be given to people who deserved them. Gifts were given to worthy recipients. Greek and Roman writers gave lots of advice about how you could determine who was worthy of a gift so that you could give your gifts properly, to the people who really deserved them.

For thousands of years, that's how grace and gift giving worked. And then the apostle Paul came along with surprising new twist. God, the perfect gift giver, gives grace to the *unworthy*, to people who don't deserve it. This was an unprecedented and revolutionary idea—so revolutionary, in fact, that Paul forever flipped the script in how we understand grace. Today, everyone thinks about grace the way Paul did. Grace is grace because we *don't* deserve it.

And it's a message that'll preach. Countless

2. John M. G. Barclay, *Paul and the Gift* (Grand Rapids: Eerdmans, 2015).

sermons have shared this flipped message of grace: You were a sinner, unworthy of grace, but Christ died for you anyway.

We can appreciate the psychological power of this message, an appeal that explains why it's so popular among preachers and evangelists. But John Barclay points out that we're still missing what was so revolutionary about Paul's strange message of grace.

We misunderstand grace because we don't appreciate Paul's major headache as he planted churches throughout Asia Minor and around the Mediterranean Sea. The churches Paul planted were pluralistic, cosmopolitan, multiracial, and multiethnic. Paul's churches were socioeconomically diverse, full of rich and poor, patrons and slaves. How was Paul going to get these very diverse communities to get along? That was Paul's big headache.

The schism that ran through every one of Paul's congregations was honor and shame. The division within the churches was between the superior and the inferior. We've already seen this in the epistle of James and 1 Corinthians 12—Christians shaming the poor and the "less honorable." Contempt was killing Paul's churches. Instead of welcoming and extending hospitality to each other, Paul's churches were divided and struggling.

What we fail to appreciate about Paul's message

of grace, according to Barclay, was the social nightmare Paul was dealing with. Consider the famous declaration from Galatians 3:28: "There is neither Jew nor Gentile, neither slave nor free, nor is there male and female, for you are all one in Christ Jesus." As modern Westerners, we think the issue in this text is political equality. True, the contrast between free and enslaved and male and female, especially in that world, maps onto our understanding of oppressor and oppressed. But that doesn't explain the Jew/Gentile relationship. Jews weren't oppressing Gentiles.

The contrast between male/female, slave/free, and Jew/Gentile wasn't political equality. The distinction was honor and shame, superior versus inferior. Females, slaves, and Gentiles in Paul's churches stood in the inferior, shameful position relative to males, Roman citizens, and ethnic Jews.

The scandal of Paul's message of grace was that grace was poured out upon these inferior, shameful people, upon those deemed to be unworthy. Grace obliterated how Paul's churches divided up the winners and the losers, the honored and shamed. Grace was poured out upon all, irrespective of social position. Grace destroyed the pecking order: "You are all one in Christ."

Grace is a social revolution. Grace clears the table so hospitality can flow.

In Ephesians, Paul describes the "wall of hostility" that was dividing the Jews and Gentiles in his churches. Grace wasn't just a spiritual issue for Paul. Grace solved a social problem. Two groups of people who scorned each other were sitting in the same pews. A wall was at work here, but it wasn't a wall made of concrete and bricks. It was an emotional wall—a wall of feelings, a wall of contempt. Grace, Paul preaches, tears down this wall of hostility.

We all think dark thoughts. The wall of hostility runs through every heart. We feel contempt for huge swaths of the world. We see a news report about people who vote differently from us, who have a different skin color than us, dress differently than us, worship a different god than us, speak a different language than us. In them, our stranger God is seeking us, but God cannot reach us through the walls of snobbery, superiority, scorn, contempt, and disdain that we erect between ourselves and the world.

So this is where hospitality lives, or dies.

With that murderer in our heart.

7

BUILD THAT WALL!

A couple of years ago, I was invited to give a talk for a group working toward racial reconciliation within my faith tradition. White and black leaders from our congregations attended. There were two main talks, both presentations given by psychologists, one white and one black. The talk given by the African American psychologist was entitled "Black Rage." My talk, as the Caucasian psychologist, would follow. I was assigned "White Fear."

I took the stage and looked at my black brothers and sisters in the audience.

"Given what we've just heard about black rage in response to the history of oppression in America, from slavery to Jim Crow to Ferguson, it may be offensive to listen to a talk about 'white fear'—

especially if you consider these fears to be paranoid and delusional. To consider the feelings of white folks will seem obscene, given the legacy and ongoing oppression of black folks. Who cares about *feelings* when *oppression* is taking place?"

But my colleague Jerry Taylor, the host of the conference, felt that a talk about white fear was in order. Jerry, who is African American, knows that when it comes to hospitality, fear is one of our biggest emotional battlegrounds.

When our hearts are gripped by fear, the will to embrace evaporates. And not just in race relations. In a world of terrorist attacks and economic insecurity, fear cripples our ability to welcome the God who comes to us in foreigners, refugees, and immigrants.

ANOTHER BRICK IN THE WALL

When Donald Trump publicly announced his run for president in 2015, he made few remarks about Mexico: "The U.S. has become a dumping ground for everybody else's problems. . . . When Mexico sends its people, they're not sending their best. They're not sending you. . . . They're sending people that have lots of problems. . . . They're bringing drugs. They're bringing crime. They're rapists."[1]

Trump's signature promise as a candidate, right from the start, was building a wall across the entire length of the US/Mexico border. "I would build a great wall," Trump said. "Nobody builds walls better than me."

When politicians paint a vision of foreigners, immigrants, and refugees as drug traffickers, rapists, and people with "lots of problems," putting a wall between these dark hordes and your loved ones seems very reasonable. Hand me a brick!

Fear and walls go hand in hand—and not just in American politics, in our churches as well. Many churches try hard to be hospitable. But when "those people" start showing up in the pews, members grow anxious and uncomfortable. I've seen it happen in church after church. A fog of fear starts to descend upon the congregation. In my experience, the number-one worry expressed when the wrong sorts of people start showing up on Sunday is this: Are our kids going to be safe?

Strangers makes us anxious. Are my kids safe? Will that immigrant take my job? Is that woman in a hijab a terrorist? Is that black teenager in a hoodie going to mug me?

1. "Here's Donald Trump's Presidential Announcement Speech," *Time*, June 16, 2015, http://time.com/3923128/donald-trump-announcement-speech.

In our political and social-media debates, we argue about whether the threats we face are real or illusory, legitimate or grossly exaggerated. But the point I'm making here is one from Psychology 101: Fear and walls go hand in hand, like peanut butter and jelly.

And walls make hospitality impossible.

THE POWER OF THE DEVIL

A lot of Christians feel awkward talking about the devil. We're too scientific and sophisticated, we think, to be worried about the Prince of Darkness. But in my book *Reviving Old Scratch: Demons and the Devil for Doubters and the Disenchanted*, I point out why we need to start talking a whole lot more about the devil. We live in culture saturated and driven by fear. We worry about our nation, our borders, our jobs, our schools, our neighborhoods, our values, our way of life. But fear, the book of Hebrews tells us, is the power of the devil. Hebrews 2:14–15 describes the devil's hold on us as a lifelong *slavery to fear*. The devil gets his claws into us when we get lost in the fog of anxiety, suspicion, paranoia, and worry about those people with strange accents, customs, and skin colors.

This fear of strangers is often triggered by

scarcity. Brené Brown describes scarcity as "the never enough problem": "Scarcity thrives in a culture where everyone is hyperaware of lack. Everything from safety and love to money and resources feels restricted or lacking."[2] Scarcity fuels our suspicion of strangers. When our paychecks feel vulnerable, we worry about immigrants taking our jobs. When safety feels scarce, we build walls around our nation and put gates around our communities.

Beyond a feeling of lack, scarcity is also a feeling of loss. We think back to the good ol' days, back to a time of happiness, goodness, safety, strength, and abundance. As we watch the news today, everything seems so much worse by comparison. Our nostalgia comes with a feeling of decay. The world has changed for the worse: the jobs more precarious, the threats more dangerous, the people less virtuous, the kids less respectful, the future more ominous.

My talk about "white fear" focused on this feeling of nostalgia. Politicians play to our fears by painting a picture of a lost Golden Age, a time not so long ago when our neighborhoods were safe, the sidewalks clean, and the nation powerful and prosperous. This idyllic, but highly selective, vision of mowed lawns and white picket fences is followed up

2. Brené Brown, *Daring Greatly* (New York: Gotham, 2012), 22.

with stories of decline and ruin. Everything we cherish and love, we are told, is fading away or being attacked.

An important part of this narrative of loss and threat is finding someone to blame for it all. We need a scapegoat. And given their strange ways and accents, strangers are perfectly suited for this purpose.

This is how the devil uses fear to turn us against each other. After World War I, Germany suffered from a crushing and prolonged recession. Hunger was widespread. Nostalgia for the good ol' days was at a fever pitch. And in the middle of that climate of fear and scarcity, Hitler pointed the finger at the Jews. Fearful and anxious as Germans were about tomorrow, Hitler gave his nation a scapegoat. And the devil sprang his trap.

PERFECT LOVE CASTS OUT FEAR

If fear is the power of the devil, perfect love casts out fear (1 John 4:18). Instead of xenophobia, the fear of strangers, hospitality is *philoxenia*, the love of strangers (Hebrews 13:2; Romans 12:13). Hospitality is the exorcism of fear.

I can hear the objection: Aren't there real risks

out there? Not all walls are bad. Even the kindest people lock their doors at night.

When it comes to hospitality, the issue isn't the walls but the fear. Our battle with the devil is a battle against fearing strangers, for three reasons.

First, fear affects our ability to assess threat and danger accurately. Fear causes us to overestimate risk. Fear makes us paranoid and suspicious. Consequently, our fears can become delusional and disconnected from reality. We begin seeing monsters under the bed and a bogeyman in the closet. When the fog of fear descends, we see enemies in the faces of friends, and threats where none exist. The devil is, after all, the Father of Lies. And most of the lies he tells us are about strangers.

The second problem with fear is dehumanization. There was a lot of outrage when Donald Trump said Mexican immigrants were rapists. But perhaps the most troubling thing he said that day was this: "They are not sending you." The implication is clear: Those people are not like us.

Fear transforms strangers into monsters, into something dangerously less than human. Monsters are bestial and animalistic. Monsters are created when our fear of strangers mixes with disgust. The infamous Nazi propaganda film *The Eternal Jew* superimposed images of Jews with rats. Members of the Westboro Baptist Church have carried signs saying, "Fags Are Beasts." The people we fear become a source of filth and degradation. So we need a wall between us and them.

But we've watched too many monster movies to feel comfortable with the story. Who is the real beast in Disney's *Beauty and the Beast*? It's not the beast, but the guy screaming, "Kill the beast!" Who is the real monster, Frankenstein or the mob carrying pitchforks? It's just like Nietzsche once warned: Beware that, when fighting monsters, you yourself do not become a monster. That's what happened in Germany. Fear doesn't just build walls. Fear turns *us* into the monsters. We become the mob carrying the pitchforks.

Finally, for Christians, the last reason we battle against fear is the most important. We cast out fear because love is risky, especially sacrificial love.

God's love didn't play it safe with us. Neither should our love. In loving us, God got hurt. Love opens us up to heartbreak and even harm. The symbol of our faith isn't a wall, but a cross.

Jesus was crucified because of love, and Jesus asks his followers to take up their own crosses to follow him. Hebrews 11:35–37 describes the early followers of Jesus this way: "[They] were tortured. . . . Some faced jeers and flogging, and even chains and imprisonment. They were put to death by stoning; they were sawed in two; they were killed by the sword."

The early Christians weren't interested in playing it safe. Perfect love casts out fear.

When you're carrying a cross, you don't have much time for walls.

8

HEART TRIGGERS

"Wait, you have *bedbugs?*"

I asked this with some alarm because Robert and Judy were sitting in my car. I was taking them home again after church. On this particular night, Robert and Judy casually shared with me their bedbug problems. Like many at Freedom, Robert and Judy live in a low-income apartment complex. Bedbug infestations seem to move around these apartment complexes like a virus during flu season.

Let me confess here, I have some OCD issues, so Robert and Judy's bedbugs were freaking me out. The two of them were, after all, sitting in my car, and they don't regularly wash their clothes. So I was worried that bedbugs had been transported into my car and that I'd carry them into my house.

This is still an issue for me, but I know that if

I want to widen the circle of my affections, then I might pick up some bedbugs.

What actually triggers the social emotions of disgust, contempt, and fear varies a lot. What makes me uncomfortable might not bother you at all, and vice versa. I have OCD triggers, so the prospect of getting bedbugs affects me a lot, tempting me to back away from some people and situations. Instead of leaning into the relationship, I find myself leaning away. I'm not mean or hostile, just more standoffish and withdrawn—less hospitable. The circle of my affections narrows.

By contrast, I have friends who have political triggers. Who you voted for in the last election can make them very upset, causing them to back away from you with disgust and anger. While I have bedbug issues, I'm less emotional about politics. I'm very relaxed talking to people across the political spectrum.

If we want to widen the circle of our affections, we need to do more than name the negative feelings we have toward people. We need to observe and inventory what triggers these emotions. These triggers are the emotional battleground of hospitality. When we're emotionally triggered, we need to be intentional in holding onto the will to embrace.

That's the first thing hospitality demands of us, the first shot in the battle being waged in our hearts.

Let's go on a tour of heart triggers, places where we find our feelings of disgust, contempt, and fear rising up, where we find the circle of our affections collapsing. Though not exhaustive, this tour is simply an attempt to help us become more self-reflective, to think about where we struggle to show hospitality. Let's do some self-assessment and self-analysis. What are your triggers? What causes you to avoid or exclude people? The discipline of hospitality begins right there.

POLITICS

Let's jump right into one of the biggest emotional triggers of all. How do you feel about people who vote differently from you?

A few years ago, I was talking about hospitality at a church in California. After worship, many of the members excitedly approached me. "Susan hugged Jack!" they exclaimed. Everyone seemed really excited about this hug. Something icy had melted between these two, but it took me a few conversations to figure out the backstory.

Susan had grown up in the 1960s. She was a flower child, a hippie, a lifelong feminist and progressive activist. She was about as liberal as a liberal Californian could be. Jack, by contrast, was about the same age, but he was a wealthy Tea Party Republican and businessman.

Despite going to the same church, Susan never spoke to Jack. In fact, she disliked and resented him. The wall of hostility was at work. As a wealthy Republican businessman, Jack looked to Susan like the enemy, the cause of everything that was wrong in the world. Jack was the Problem.

But the church and I had spent the entire morning talking about how hospitality begins with welcoming people into the circle of our affections, and how that begins by leaning into relationships when we'd rather lean away. Something in the conversation connected with Susan, so after church, she approached Jack and said, "I think I need to hug you." And they hugged. After years of going to church together, Susan and Jack hugged for the very first time. The flower child hugged the businessman. Susan had leaned in and widened the circle of her affections to include Jack.

HABITS AND LIFESTYLE

What do you think of smokers? Or of people who shop at Walmart and eat at McDonald's? What do you think of vegans? How about hunters and gun owners? How do you feel about people who home-school their kids? People who drive SUVs? People who drink alcohol? People who don't drink?

Think of any habit or lifestyle choice that you find disgusting, weird, pretentious, or objectionable, then ponder your feelings about the people you encounter who are engaging in these things. Every habit, behavior, or lifestyle choice can be a trigger that causes us to lean away from people—locations where we experience revulsion, anger, or contempt.

For example, at Freedom Fellowship, a lot of our members have histories with substance use and are in recovery. And you find a lot of smokers among people in recovery. So before and after our meals and services at Freedom, a lot of our members go outside to smoke.

Smoking is a habit that can trigger people. Many people think smoking is disgusting, and this affects how they look at smokers. Plus, in a lot of churches, smoking is considered a sin. So smokers are not only disgusting and unhealthy, they are also bad people.

But if you want to walk alongside people on the long road toward recovery, as well as welcome people across socioeconomic lines, you're going to have to deal with your feelings about smoking. In my opin-ion, you can tell how hospitable a church is by counting the number of smokers outside on a Sunday morning.

HYGIENE

I've already mentioned my bedbug issues. But there are many other hygiene-related triggers that you'll encounter when you try to welcome people at the very bottom of the socioeconomic ladder, especially the homeless. During the summers here in Texas, when many of our family at Freedom don't have the luxury of a shower, the pungent body odors in the auditorium can become overwhelming. For some people, these smells are really triggering, to the point of nausea.

When Jesus says he comes to us disguised as a homeless person, we fail to appreciate that Jesus will *stink*. And we fail to see Jesus because the smells are blinding us.

A few years ago in their hometown of Itu, Brazil, my dear friends Mark and Ali Kaiser began welcoming people living on the streets into their home for a simple meal of rice and beans. Sometimes the body odors were so strong that Ali struggled with her gag reflex as she cooked. But Mark and Ali pushed past the smells, eventually giving ownership of the meal over to their homeless neighbors. Empowered neighbors soon became friends. These friendships led Mark and Ali to open Crescimento Limpo (Portuguese for "Clean Growth"), where they provide housing and substance-use counseling for the residents.[1]

That's what can happen in the kingdom of God when you don't let your gag reflex determine the circle of your affections.

APPEARANCE

There's a famous finding in psychology called "What is beautiful is good."[2] Basically, attractive people are perceived to be more intelligent and more virtuous than less attractive people. And conversely, ugly people are thought to be less intelligent and more immoral. As children, we're told over and over again not to judge a book by its cover. And yet we do.

A lot of my friends at Freedom don't have any teeth because they lack adequate dental care. Not having teeth affects your appearance. When you don't have any teeth, you can't smile, and when you can't smile, you look mean and sinister. And people

---

1. You can learn more about the good work being done at Crescimento Limpo at the organization's English-language website, http://crescimentolimpo.org.br/us.
2. Karen Dion, Ellen Berscheid, and Elaine Walster, "What Is Beautiful Is Good," *Journal of Personality and Social Psychology* 24 (1972): 285–90.

don't lean in when they see someone looking mean and sinister.

Think also about tattoos and body piercings, haircuts and hair colors, and clothing choices, from high heels to cowboy boots to baggy pants. We are constantly sizing people up, leaning toward or away from them, based upon what they look like and what they're wearing.

DISABILITIES

When we see someone with a disability, we often feel compassion. But we can also feel uncomfortable. If you see a child with cerebral palsy in a wheelchair, you may want to lean in, but you hesitate, thinking you need some special medical or nursing skill to know what to do in an interaction. People with disabilities and parents of children with disabilities find this silly. No special medical skill is needed to say hello, to have a conversation and offer an affectionate touch. Yet, we hesitate, feeling awkward.

After weeks of sitting with us in church, Kristi started coming to our adult Bible class. The first day she came, Kristi asked if someone could take her to the bathroom. I'm a man, so I asked the class for help. As you can imagine, Kristi's wheelchair and blindness caused some hesitation. But Kathleen said yes, she'd help. What did she need to do? It was no big deal. Kristi's pretty independent. She just needed a push to an open stall.

What began with hesitancy and awkwardness that day has now become normal and routine for our class. Many women now help Kristi. But it started with one person, Kathleen, saying yes.

DEMOGRAPHICS

Ponder all the ways we're triggered by race, sexual orientation, religion, and nationality: minorities, LGBT persons, Muslims, immigrants, refugees.

Jana, my wife, loves to shop at thrift stores. When you buy your clothing at thrift stores, you need to know a good alterations place. You can't always get the perfect size at the local Goodwill.

The woman at Jana's favorite alterations shop was from Cambodia. After a few visits, Jana asked for her name. "Ruthie," she said. And from that small beginning, a wonderful friendship was born.

It seems like a small thing, making the effort to get on a first-name basis with someone, but it's a bridge few of us make the effort to cross, especially across the lines of ethnicity and nationality. Ruthie's English is very broken, something that embarrasses her, so she's very quiet. People have gone to Ruthie for years, but few have taken the time to get to know the lady crawling around on the floor, pinning their hemlines.

The backstory of Jana's desire to connect with Ruthie began on the killing fields of Cambodia. From 1975 to 1979, Pol Pot and the Khmer Rouge killed between one and a half million and three million people in the Cambodian genocide. Many Cambodian refugees fled to the United States, and some made their way to Texas. Jana's father, Pat, was the pastor of a small church in Dallas. One day, Pat's phone rang, asking if his church could help with the influx of Cambodian refugees. Pat and the church said yes, they would sponsor some of the refugees.

So Jana grew up among the Cambodians—helping to teach English classes, making friends, and going to the church her father helped the Cambodians start. White, evangelical Texans welcomed the refugees.

I came late to this story. On our wedding day, on Jana's side of the aisle, I saw a huge Cambodian crowd. Among the poorest of our guests, they gave some of the most lavish gifts. Cambodians are great gift givers. The other day, Jana took our son Aidan in to get his pants hemmed. Ruthie gave him a watermelon. "Why did she give me a watermelon?" our puzzled son asked. "Because," said Jana, "Ruthie and I are friends."

It was no accident Jana leaned in to learn Ruthie's name. It had started decades before, when her father, a Texas pastor, answered the call to help the refugees.

SOCIAL SKILLS

Some people are weird or irritating. If you were a *Seinfeld* fan, do you remember the episode with the guy who was a close talker? You know the type, a person who stands too close to you, invading your personal space in face-to-face conversations.

A list of social-skill problems that annoy us would be endless: close talkers, people who name-drop, people who talk too much about themselves, who don't make eye contact, who laugh too loud, who linger too long, who don't take hints or no for an answer. Then there are people who are overly sensitive or insensitive and people who are sickly sweet or rude. A lot of our emotional reactions toward people are in response to their social skills or personality quirks. Some people are witty, fun, interesting, and charismatic. We lean into these people. But other people bore and annoy us. We lean away, ignoring them, or treating them brusquely and rudely.

SINS, CRIMES, AND MORAL FAILURES

When I was growing up, I was told that all sins were equally bad in the sight of God. Maybe so, but humans sure don't feel that way.

I don't think we appreciate the shock of what it meant that Jesus welcomed tax collectors. Tax collectors were Jewish agents who worked for the Romans, the hated enemies who occupied the Jewish homeland. Tax collectors took money from their fellow Jews and handed it over to the Romans. The tax collectors were traitors. And patriots hate traitors.

Let me put it this way. How do you feel about Americans who have gone over to the Middle East to fight with the Taliban or ISIS? Imagine if a nation like China or Russia defeated and occupied the American homeland. How would you feel about the Americans who worked for the occupying forces against fellow Americans? I suspect you'd feel a very strong sense of betrayal. As a patriot, you'd hate these traitors. You'd be revolted and sickened by them—just like the Jews felt about the tax collectors.

Yet Jesus was known as a friend of tax collectors, counting one of them among his closest associates.

Whenever people do things that we consider morally outrageous, we have a hard time welcoming them into the circle of our affections.

The inmates I see each week know how people "in the free world" feel about them. The Men in White know that society thinks they are despicable and beyond redemption. They feel that hostility. And the recently paroled know what's going to happen when they check that box on every job application, the box declaring that they have a felony conviction. They aren't going to get that call for a second interview.

Personal History

"I want to apologize."

Darell and I go to the same church. A few years ago, Darell and I had a disagreement in a meeting. We didn't know each other at the time, so the small argument we had was our first and only interaction. But that first negative—mild but negative—interaction colored our relationship from that day forward. We never sought each other out; we never went out of our way to have another, more positive interaction. We weren't being mean or hostile; we just were leaning away from each other. You've probably had a similar experience.

Years later, we found ourselves at Freedom Fellowship, where we had the chance to get to know each other. The ice was broken when Darell came over to me one night. "I want to apologize," Darell said. "We had that little argument years ago, and after that argument, I assumed you were arrogant. But I was mistaken." I wasn't the one who took the initiative to hit the reset button between us. Darell was the bigger, better man. For that grace, I'm thankful. Darell and I are now great friends.

A lot of what separates us is the bad experiences we have with each other. We feel slighted, dismissed, or belittled in an interaction, and we nurse resentment for months, years, and decades. Based on one unpleasant interaction, we label a person arrogant or a jerk, and from that point forward, we start leaning away. There was no reason Darell and I couldn't have been friends years earlier. But a tiny little grudge had narrowed the circle of our affections, and that was all it took for us to ignore each other.

This tour of heart triggers could go on and on, with many more examples. But all I've been trying to impress upon you are all the different ways we are emotionally triggered to lean away from people, and how these triggers are the emotional battleground of hospitality. If we're going to widen the circle of our affections, these are the locations where that battle must be waged, because in the face of each trigger, our hearts shrink and pull back. The discipline of hospitality begins with a deep and honest survey of all those places where we emotionally withdraw from people, followed by the commitment, in the face of these triggers, to start leaning in.

9

JESUS, YOU ARE MAKING ME TIRED

"I saw the word *radical*, and I didn't want to come today."

I was at a church, doing equipping sessions about welcoming and hospitality. The church had advertised the classes and sermon I was delivering as a part of what they called "Radical Hospitality Sunday."

After services, a lady came up to me. "I saw the word *radical*," she said, "and I didn't want to come to church. I just felt too tired. I didn't want to feel guilty for not doing more. I just couldn't face that today."

I've had that conversation, in some form or fashion, a hundred times. When pastors and Christian authors talk about sacrificial love, authentic relationships, and hospitality, they love to use words like *radical, costly*, and *messy*. "When we love people the way Jesus loved people," they exhort, "our lives will get messy. Real, authentic relationships are complicated and hard; they demand sacrifice. Jesus is calling on us to get in the trenches of each other's lives."

It's a great pitch, this call to "radical" love. But do you know what the people are thinking when they hear about love being messy and hospitality being radical? They're thinking, "Jesus, you are making me tired."

OUR REVERIE OF LACK

People are exhausted. Our schedules are totally maxed out. We have no margin. So where are we going to find the time and energy for all this hospitality—to say nothing of *radical* hospitality?

Earlier I described how always looking for our friends is our number-one hospitality problem. Let me take that back, or at least add the leading contender. The real number-one problem for why we don't extend radical hospitality is mental and physical exhaustion. No one has any time or energy.

That's the complaint I hear over and over again whenever I speak about hospitality. I ask audiences,

"What's the biggest thing keeping you from investing more in relationships with others?" And the answer is always the same: time. People just don't have enough time to devote to messy, complicated relationships. We're all too busy for a life of radical hospitality.

Our lives are dominated by those feelings of scarcity. In her book *Daring Greatly*, Brené Brown shares this assessment from Lynne Twist:

> *For me, and for many of us, our first waking thought of the day is "I didn't get enough sleep." The next one is "I don't have enough time." Whether true or not, that thought of not enough occurs to us automatically before we even think to question or examine it. . . . Before we even sit up in bed, before our feet touch the floor, we're already inadequate, already behind, already losing, already lacking something. And by the time we go to bed at night, our minds are racing with a litany of what we didn't get, or didn't get done, that day. We go to sleep burdened by those thoughts and wake up to that reverie of lack.*[1]

It's hard to call people to a life of radical hospitality when our lives are governed by a "reverie of lack." If

1. Brené Brown, *Daring Greatly* (New York: Gotham, 2012), 25–26.

hospitality is all about making room, what are we to do when we feel like we don't have any more room in our lives?

The examples that Christians often use to illustrate radical hospitality fill us with both awe and dread. We feel awe for the radical and heroic witnesses we see around us—people doing amazing and sacrificial things for the kingdom of God. These followers of Jesus excite us, but they also scare us or make us feel guilty. We have day jobs, a mortgage, and our kid's soccer game to coach this evening. Plus, our marriage is hanging by a thread. And work is burying us. We've got a lot of stuff on our plates.

A MILLION BORING LITTLE THINGS

We exhaust ourselves because we think being like Jesus means performing more and more good deeds. So hospitality becomes one of those good deeds to add to our weekend To Do list. Invite people over. Clean the house. Cook a meal. Entertain and host. Clean it all up afterward.

Or we think hospitality is a service project, a form of volunteerism. We stack cans at the food bank. We cook a meal for the soup kitchen. We sort clothing for the clothing drive. We mow a lawn during a service weekend. We bring a casserole for the potluck. We set out tables for the neighborhood cookout. We hand out turkeys at Thanksgiving. If that is what we mean by hospitality, to say nothing of *radical* hospitality, no wonder the prospect of hospitality intimidates us. Hospitality isn't sustainable if it is a long list of good deeds we have to perform, year after year after year.

But hospitality isn't an afternoon at the food bank or a dinner you cook. When Jana introduced herself to Ruthie, she wasn't thinking about Ruthie as a service project, as something to check off a spiritual To Do list. Jana was simply opening herself up to a relationship.

A few years ago, I was talking with one of my students about how we grow spiritually. "Being like Jesus," I said, "is a million boring little things"—boring little things like waiting patiently in a line, being patient with your kids, listening to your spouse, being a dependable friend.

It's the same with hospitality. Hospitality isn't a list of service projects to fill up our schedules. Hospitality is a million boring little things that expand the territory of our kindness in ways that open us up to welcoming the stranger God.

AN EMOTIONAL REVOLUTION

What does a life of radical hospitality and discipleship look like when I'm just doing my best to keep my head above water?

I don't want to suggest that there isn't something spiritually problematic with how busy we are. We really do need to make more room for each other. I think our busyness and our exhaustion are rooted in a spiritual sickness that runs throughout American society. But addressing that sickness is a big rock to lift. It's an issue we need to tackle, perhaps the biggest problem facing Western Christians, but I don't think we need to wait to get that huge problem fixed before we can turn to practices of hospitality.

If hospitality is, at root, widening the circle of our affections, then it's not a practice that adds anything to an already-full life. What I am describing is a revolution of our emotions. Hospitality isn't about adding something to your already packed To Do list. Hospitality is, rather, welcoming and being with the people already in our lives: the people at work, the people in your neighborhood, and the people in your kid's soccer league. It's the way Jana got to know Ruthie.

Yes, when you widen circle of your affections, you will welcome new people into your life. God will come to you in strangers. And those strangers will often become your friends. But that's the magic trick we're looking for. Hospitality isn't volunteerism, a service project to add to your list of responsibilities. Hospitality is availability and openness to unexpected and surprising friendships. Friendships, because we desire them and because they are filled with mutual joy, don't feel like a burden or a To Do list. Friends aren't service projects. True friendship is mutual, support given back and forth. Yes, friendships can get messy, but in ways that bring us together and pick us up. Friends help each other. Jana is a drama teacher, and Ruthie has saved her bacon many times with a costume fix. Friends like Ruthie make life easier and lighter to carry. They even give you watermelons.

My life has been blessed by welcoming the Men in White and friends like Miss Beth at Freedom. I run to these relationships for support. I need them. These unlikely friendships have saved me.

Remember, *God* is coming to us in strangers. What we are welcoming into our lives isn't a burden or a drain. When we widen the circle of our affections, we are welcoming grace and joy and love.

And who doesn't have room for that?

PART III

"I SHALL BE
LOVE"

10

SEARCHING FOR THE SCIENCE OF LOVE

She died when she was twenty-four, after a prolonged and painful illness. By all outward appearances, her life had been unremarkable—less than unremarkable, really. One of the sisters who had lived with her in the convent for many years wondered aloud, "Are we going to have anything to say about her at the funeral?"

That's how ordinary she seemed—no highlights or accomplishments to share at her memorial service. She was sweet and kind, it was universally agreed, but she had not distinguished herself. She had died young and had done nothing with her life that anyone had noticed or would remember.

Last week, I pondered this reaction to her death and chuckled to myself. I was in San Antonio, standing in a beautiful basilica dedicated to her memory.

She's the Little Flower, one of the most popular saints in Catholicism: Saint Thérèse of Lisieux.

I guess they found some stuff to say about her, after all.

HUNTING HOSPITALITY

For my part, I found Thérèse out of desperation. In 2011, I had published a book entitled *Unclean* about a lot of the material I covered in part 2. Because of that book, people began to call, asking me to come and talk about the social psychology of hospitality. I'd show up and talk about disgust and contempt, about spitting in Dixie cups and poop touching apples. I'd talk about the moral circle, the will to embrace, and about how hospitality is widening the circle of our affections to welcome the Jesus who comes to us in disguise. I'd talk about the strangeness of the God who comes to us in strangers. Basically, I'd talk about everything in this book right up to this sentence.

And after I had done all that, someone would raise a hand and ask a very natural question: "So how should we do what you are suggesting? If all this emotional triggering is going on in our hearts, how can we change it?"

Great question! But I didn't have an answer. I'd say something like, "Well, I'm not an expert in spiritual formation. I'm an experimental psychologist. I'm just describing the psychological challenges we face as we try to welcome people." Which, let's be honest, is a really terrible answer. I was punting.

(Sad to say, but academics like me do this all the time when we talk to non-academic audiences. We talk about ideas and theories, and then, when it's time to get practical, we say, "Well, I'm a *scholar*, not a *practitioner*." I was embarrassed that I was playing this card.)

I found my lack of an answer so personally upsetting that I began to search the spiritual formation and hospitality literature for something—anything!—practical to say. During my search, I had two criteria firmly in mind that this spiritual practice had to satisfy. Two criteria and a personal commitment.

The first criterion was this: Whatever I was looking for had to be an intentional practice, a habit-forming spiritual discipline. The reason for this is simple and goes to the whole point of this book. If hospitality starts with our affections, then hospitality isn't ever going to begin with a new program or policy. Hospitality never starts with a new welcoming initiative that's looking for volunteers or a law to be passed by voters. Programs and policies can bring people into physical proximity, but if our hearts aren't changed, we can live right next to each other and still never cross the bridge to friendship. Programs and policies can bring bodies into closer contact, but we can still refuse to make ourselves emotionally available to welcome Jesus in disguise. Plus, the main reason social and economic policy proposals are rejected is that we lack friendships with the people being adversely affected by the status quo. Changing policy requires a change of heart. We're back in the emotional trenches.

All that to say, I wasn't on the lookout for a new program or policy fix. I was looking for a habit-forming practice that could change our hearts and lead us into unexpected and surprising friendships.

And while looking for this practice, I wasn't searching the bookshelves of Christian bookstores for more amazing examples of radical hospitality to point to and say, "Be like these people." Pointing to an example isn't a practice. That's like pointing at an NBA star and demanding, "Shoot three-pointers like him!" Not going to happen. An NBA player has shot a basketball in a gym for decades—thousands upon thousands of practice shots. You can't pick up a basketball for the first time and shoot like a NBA star.

Hospitality, as an affectional capacity, is exactly the same. You have to practice your way, slowly and over time, into a wider circle of affections. Having a "Radical Hospitality Sunday" to launch a new welcoming or neighboring initiative won't make people more hospitable, nor will a great sermon or passing a new law. Our affections can't be rewired so quickly.

My second criterion had to do with what we discussed in chapter 9—our feelings of exhaustion. I needed to find a spiritual practice that didn't add to our overscheduled lives but could be practiced *within* our lives—a practice anyone could do, no matter how busy they were. No excuses.

Along with those two criteria, I added a personal commitment that I would adopt the practice for myself. Before I told people to take this practice out on the road, I wanted to test-drive it. I wanted to make sure the practice would work, and I wanted to have examples of how the practice had helped me widen the circle of my own affections.

So I began my search. I began scouring the Christian literature on hospitality. I read the memoirs of people whose lives displayed remarkable hospitality, but I couldn't find anything that didn't reduce to the simple command to be more hospitable or point to a radical exemplar of hospitality with the encouragement to imitate him or her, all of which amounted to the hospitality equivalent of "Everyone, start shooting and making three-pointers like you're in the NBA!"

However, during my searches, the name of Thérèse of Lisieux kept popping up, especially in the Catholic writings about hospitality. Some people I really admired, like Mother (now Saint) Teresa of Calcutta, Thomas Merton, and Dorothy Day, said they had been affected by what they called Thérèse's "Little Way." In fact, Mother Teresa took her name from Thérèse of Lisieux, opting for the Spanish spelling. Dorothy Day was a radical practitioner of hospitality as the founder of the Catholic Worker Movement. Working out of their Houses of Hospitality, the Catholic Workers remain some of the most committed practitioners of hospitality in the world today. And Dorothy Day, I discovered, had written a biography of Thérèse of Lisieux. I figured if Mother Teresa of Calcutta and Dorothy Day were in your corner, you were worth taking a look at. So, after months of reading, I turned to the life and witness of Thérèse of Lisieux and her practice of the Little Way.

The Story of a Soul

Thérèse Martin was born on January 2, 1873, in Alençon, France. Her parents were devout Catholics, Louis and Zelie Martin. The family had a very high view of monastic life, as both parents had tried in their early lives to join a monastic community. Eventually, two of Thérèse's older sisters, Pauline and Marie, entered the cloistered Carmelite convent in Lisieux, Normandy.

Thérèse herself was spiritually precocious and wanted to follow her sisters into the Carmelites, but she chafed at having to wait until the required sixteen years of age. She eventually petitioned Pope Leo XIII for a special dispensation to enter the convent early. This was granted, and on April 9, 1888, at the age of fifteen, Thérèse joined her sisters.

From all external perspectives, Thérèse's years at Carmel were quiet and uneventful. She dutifully participated in the life of the community, but without outward distinction. She loved to write, often composing plays that were performed by the sisters.

In the early morning of Good Friday 1896, Thérèse awoke to find her mouth full of blood. She struggled with tuberculosis for well over a year, and then, after two days of great pain, Thérèse died on September 30, 1897. She was twenty-four.

In 1925, a mere twenty-eight years after her death, Pope Pius XI presided over Thérèse's canonization. Since then, Thérèse has become one of the most popular of the Catholic saints, with huge worldwide devotion. Pius X called Thérèse "the greatest saint of modern times." In 1997, Pope John Paul II named Thérèse a doctor of the church, putting her in rarefied air in the company of people like Augustine and Thomas Aquinas. In the Catholic Church, a doctor of the church is someone whose teachings are considered to be exemplary and to cast new light upon the faith. Only four women are doctors of the church: Teresa of Avila, Catherine of Siena, Hildegard of Bingen, and Thérèse of Lisieux.

What is striking here is the contrast between Thérèse's undistinguished life and her posthumous fame and influence. What happened?

The impact of Thérèse rests upon the influence of her spiritual memoir, published after her death —*Story of a Soul* (or *Histoire d'une Ame* in French).

Story of a Soul was published the year after Thérèse's death, and much to the surprise of her Carmelite sisters, it gained widespread notoriety. During her life, few around Thérèse sensed that a spiritual hurricane was raging inside of her, that the quiet and humble exterior was hiding, in the assessment of Pope John Paul II, "one of the great masters of the spiritual life in our time."

But the magic of *Story of a Soul* can be hard to find. While it's true that many have been profoundly affected by *Story of a Soul*, it's also true that some people don't like the book and can't see what all the fuss is about. This was the first reaction Dorothy Day had toward the book. Here is how Day described her first encounter with *Story of a Soul*:

> *My confessor at the time was Father Zachary. . . . He was preparing me for Confirmation, giving me weekly evening instruction.*

> *One day Father Zachary said to me, "Here is a book that will do you good." . . . The book he now handed me was* The Little Flower: The Story of a Soul. . . .

> *I dutifully read* The Story of a Soul *and am ashamed to confess that I found it colorless, monotonous, too small in fact for my notice. . . . I was reading in my Daily Missal of saints stretched on the rack, burnt by flames, starving themselves in the desert, and so on. . . . Joan of Arc leading an army fitted more into my concept of a saint. . . . I wondered what this new saint had to offer. . . . It took me a*

long time to realize the unique position of Thérèse of Lisieux in the Church today.[1]

Dorothy Day was like a lot of my college students—all fired up and looking for heroic and radical ways of following Jesus in the world. If that's what you're looking for, your first encounter with the Little Way of Thérèse might be unsatisfying. For all the aspiring heroes out there, the Little Way does indeed seem very little. But the little disciplines of the Little Way packs a nuclear-sized punch. Dorothy Day was eventually convinced and became a devotee of Thérèse. After being converted to the Little Way, Day wrote, "Is the atom a small thing? And yet what havoc it has wrought. Is her little way a small contribution to the life of the Spirit? It has all the power of the Spirit of Christianity behind it. It has an explosive force that can transform our lives and the life of the world, once put into effect."[2]

It's not just the smallness of the Little Way that can get in your way in reading *Story of a Soul*. As Dorothy Day noted, the writing of *Story of a Soul* can be described as colorless and monotonous. And there are parts of *Story of a Soul* that are overly

1. Dorothy Day, *Thérèse* (Notre Dame, IN: Christian Classics, 2016), xiii, xv.
2. Ibid., 192.

sentimental and sweet. It can be hard to read love-drunk contemplatives when they describe their rapturous and mystical encounters with Jesus. Thérèse tends to go ALL CAPS! when writing about HOW MUCH SHE LOVES JESUS!

All that has to be balanced out as you read and sift through *Story of a Soul*. So be advised. But as Dorothy Day and Mother Teresa can attest, it's worth the effort to discover the Little Way. As the best-selling Jesuit author James Martin describes in his book *My Life with the Saints*:

> *Though there are parts of her story that I find difficult to accept (her childhood religiosity can sound pretentious, precious, and even a little neurotic, and her efforts at self-denial sometimes are close to masochistic), and though it is embarrassing to admit that one of my favorite saints is one of the most girlish and cloying, it is finally the woman herself who appeals to me. Like every other saint, Thérèse Martin was a product of her times, raised in the overheated environment of a super-religious family and formed in the pious nineteenth-century French convent life. So it is hardly surprising that some of her words and actions occasionally baffle us. But shining through the nineteenth-century piety, like a pale green shoot*

bursting through dark soil, is a stunningly original personality, a person who, despite the difficulties of life, holds out to us her Little Way and says to us one thing: Love.[3]

But love is hard. It's often not natural. We don't just fall out of bed in the morning as loving people. And you can't demand that people become more loving, just as you can't demand that people shoot NBA three-pointers. Love takes attention and intention. It takes discipline and practice to widen the circle of our affections.

And that's exactly what I found in the Little Way. It was everything I was looking for.

Thérèse called it *the science of love.*

---

3. James Martin, *My Life with the Saints* (Chicago: Loyola, 2006), 40.

11

THE HEART OF THE CHURCH

When it comes to following Jesus, a lot of us feel trapped by our lives. We have bills to pay, aging parents to care for, a marriage to nurture, friends to keep, a car to get inspected, a work deadline to meet, a medical procedure to face, children to raise, a lawn to mow, a game to coach, clothing to fold, a bathroom to clean, dishes to wash.

Then we hear about all these amazing, heroic, sacrificial, and radical things people are doing for the kingdom of God, past and present. We hear about Saint Francis of Assisi, who renounced his family wealth. We hear about Mother Teresa, who cared for the poor in Calcutta. We also hear about radical discipleship among contemporary followers of Jesus—people in the ministries your congregation supports, people you read about on social media, people on the front lines in the battles against homelessness, sex trafficking, or poverty in the Third World. The shelves of our Christian bookstores are filled with the memoirs of these radical followers of Jesus. I recently read Father Gregory Boyle's *Tattoos on the Heart*, about his life walking alongside gang members in Los Angeles and his organization, Homeboy Industries, the largest gang outreach program in the world. The story of Father Boyle and his homeboys is wildly inspirational. You read it, and many memoirs like it, and think, "This is what following Jesus is supposed to look like!"

And then on Monday, you start your long work commute to face a pile of deadlines. Or you rush to get the kids off to school before returning home to a stack of dirty dishes and laundry to be folded.

So let's admit it. We're thrilled by stories like Father Boyle's, but we're also a bit shamed. We are pleased that there are radical stories of discipleship on the shelves of Christian bookstores. We know the world needs these stories. But these aren't *our* stories. Our days are filled with domestic life and work, and not much else. Big, heroic, and radical discipleship isn't anything we can aspire to.

So we feel like sellouts and second-rate Christians. We are standing on the sidelines watching the game, cheering others on.

The apostle Paul warned some of us about all this—how if we got married, started a family, and took out a mortgage, our loyalties would get divided between family and the kingdom of God. Radical discipleship on the one side is pitted against work and home on the other. Being an all-in radical follower of Jesus seems like a young person's game. Becoming a missionary, working for a nonprofit, or joining a nongovernmental organization in the Third World was something we dreamed about in our teens and twenties. But those dreams are now in the rearview mirror.

If you've ever felt what I'm describing, that the life you are leading at home and work doesn't have any margin for radical displays of discipleship, then you are experiencing exactly what prompted the spiritual crisis in the life of Thérèse of Lisieux, the crisis that caused her to discover the Little Way.

CRACKING THE DISCIPLESHIP CODE

Thérèse was just like us. She wanted to do big and radical things for Jesus but found herself stuck in a life that was mundane, dreary, bland, and ordinary.

Like us, Thérèse found her spiritual aspirations trapped by the smallness of her life. Thérèse lived as a cloistered nun, so the circuit of her life was fixed by the limitations and routines of monastic life.

Consequently, Thérèse's spiritual walk was dominated by the same challenges we face in our own lives: *How am I going to get along with these people?* For Thérèse, it was getting along with a group of cloistered sisters. For us, it's our collection of family, friends, coworkers, and church members. Our lives, like Thérèse's, move in a small social circle, and we spend our days working through the relational dramas on this intimate stage.

Thérèse had appealed to the pope to enter the convent a year early. She was fired up to give her life to Jesus, dreaming big dreams of radical discipleship. I suspect that Thérèse thought monastic life was going to be an amazing spiritual adventure. But what she discovered after joining the convent is what a lot of us discover after we get our first job or take out our first mortgage: Life gets trapped in routine, and we spend most of it struggling through the dramas of living with a small group of people, year after year after year.

So, like a lot of us, Thérèse had a crisis of spiritual vocation. She had wanted to do something heroic for Jesus, but her life in the convent seemed trivial and domesticated. She felt the spiritual shame and guilt we all feel, unsure what radical discipleship looked like in a life so restricted and hemmed in. For Thérèse, the restrictions were the walls and rules of the convent. Our restrictions are the walls built by full schedules, work and school deadlines, and domestic responsibilities.

Under the weight of her spiritual crisis, Thérèse fell on her knees, imploring Jesus to reveal to her what she was supposed to be doing with her life.

The story of this spiritual crisis and the answer she received occurs in the middle of her memoir, *Story of a Soul.* The revolutionary, spiritual breakthrough that Thérèse experienced is the contemplative foundation of the Little Way, the pulsating spiritual heart that animates the whole.

What we know as the *Story of a Soul* is actually three manuscripts knit together. The first part, called the "first manuscript," Thérèse wrote in 1895 for her sister Pauline, who was the prioress of the convent. One day the sisters were reminiscing about their family and childhood. Wanting to capture this, and capitalizing on Thérèse's writing ability, Pauline directed Thérèse to write about the family and her earliest memories. Thérèse dutifully did so, writing an autobiographical memoir spanning her earliest recollections to the time of her entrance into Carmel at the age of fifteen. These early chapters in *Story of a Soul* also recount the spiritual development of her early years, her immature setbacks and the advances.

The contemplative origin of the Little Way, Thérèse's big spiritual breakthrough, is found in the second manuscript. Thérèse wrote in 1896 about her revolutionary experience, in the final months of her life. She had contracted tuberculosis, and her other sister, Marie, fearing that her little sister would die before she could share her approach to the spiritual life, asked Thérèse to write down "her little doctrine."

This second manuscript is short, about twenty-four pages, only a single chapter in *Story of a Soul*. This short letter to her sister Marie contains the mystical heart of the Little Way. Many consider the testimony contained in these pages to be one of the crown jewels of the Christian contemplative tradition.

Thérèse's resolution of her vocational crisis is most brilliant because it opens up for us the possibility that anyone, no matter how small and hemmed in that person's life may be, can be a heroic and radical follower of Jesus. Thérèse cracked the discipleship code for ordinary Christians. A revolutionary life is available to each of us.

LITTLE THINGS WITH GREAT LOVE

Thérèse was struggling with her religious vocation. She had wanted to do glorious things for Jesus, but she found herself blocked by the smallness of her life. Thérèse, like a lot of us, wanted her spiritual vocation and calling in life to be heroic. In the midst of her crisis, Thérèse wrote to Jesus (in ALL CAPS!), "I feel within me other *vocations*. I feel the *vocation* of the WARRIOR, THE PRIEST, THE APOSTLE, THE DOCTOR, THE MARTYR. . . . I feel the need and the desire of carrying out the most heroic deeds for *You*."[1] Thirsting for a heroic, radical life, Thérèse was willing to do anything for Jesus: "I would shed my blood for You even to the very last drop."

But it's hard to die a martyr's death living as a cloistered nun. She was more likely to choke to death on a chicken bone than be burned at the stake. Dying like Joan of Arc, one of Thérèse's heroes, was out of the question. So, feeling trapped by the unheroic nature of her life, she wondered if God were not "asking something more of me than my poor little actions and desires. Is He content with me?"

Struggling with these feelings of guilt, Thérèse

---

1. Thérèse of Lisieux, *Story of a Soul: The Autobiography of Saint Thérèse of Lisieux*, trans. John Clarke, 3rd ed. (Washington, DC: ICS, 1996), 192.

experienced her spiritual breakthrough while reading 1 Corinthians 12–13, Paul's famous body metaphor of the church. The church, Paul says, comprises people with special gifts and vocations. Some of us are the mouth of the church—the preachers, teachers, and prophets. Some of us are the eye—leaders and vision casters. Some of us are the feet of the church—the missionaries and evangelists. Some of us are the hands of the church—the priests and pastors.

But as Thérèse read through 1 Corinthians 12, she couldn't figure out what part of the body described her. She wasn't a preacher or a missionary or a priest—not the mouth, the feet, or the hands of the church. So what was she? What part of the body? What was she supposed to be doing for Jesus?

Thérèse couldn't find anything in 1 Corinthians 12 that fit her life; no part of the body described her. And then she read on into 1 Corinthians 13, Paul's great ode to love, perhaps the most famous chapter in the Bible: "Love is patient, love is kind. . . ."

There in chapter 13, Paul makes the observation that love is greater than all the spiritual gifts. And with that insight, Thérèse had her breakthrough. Her spiritual vocation came to her in a flash. She was not the hands or the feet or the mouth or the eyes, but the heart. In the whole of the body of Christ, Thérèse laid claim to the heart.

Thérèse would become the *affections* of the church.

She would be *love*.

Thérèse expressed her realization this way:

> I finally had rest. . . . Charity gave me the key to my vocation. I understood that if the Church had a body composed of different members, the most necessary and most noble of all could not be lacking to it, and so I understood that the Church had a Heart and that this Heart is BURNING WITH LOVE. . . .
>
> Then, in the excess of my delirious joy, I cried out: O Jesus, my Love . . . my vocation, at last I have found it. . . . MY VOCATION IS LOVE!
>
> Yes, I found my place in the Church. . . . I shall be Love. Thus I shall be everything.[2]

"I shall be love"—this is the spiritual foundation of the Little Way. To practice the Little Way is to follow Thérèse's example, to be the heart, the affections of the body of Christ. The Little Way is to incarnate love in your day-to-day existence with others. No

2. Ibid., 194.

grand overseas adventures, no speaking to massive crowds, no riding off like Joan of Arc. Simply becoming love, incarnating the affections of Jesus, right here, right now.

In popular devotion, Thérèse is called the Little Flower. Thérèse compares the Little Way to strewing flowers around the throne of God, with each small act of love being a flower:

> But how will she [Thérèse is speaking in the third person] prove her love since love is proved by works? Well, the little child will strew flowers, she will perfume the royal throne with their sweet scents. . . .

> I have no other means of proving my love for you other than that of strewing flowers, that is, not allowing one little sacrifice to escape, not one look, one word, profiting by all the smallest things and doing them through love.[3]

Sentimentality aside, there is steel here, requiring a firm discipline.

Two things act in concert in the Little Way. First, the focus of the Little Way is upon actions. As Thérèse says, love is proved by works. This is why I describe the Little Way as a spiritual discipline,

3. Ibid., 196.

a habit-forming practice. Second, and most importantly, these actions are targeting our affections. The discipline of the Little Way is to make every act of sacrifice during the day, every look and every word, flow from love.

Doing little things with great love, that is the practice of the Little Way.

Can you start to appreciate the heroic audacity of the spirituality of the Little Way? When put into practice, it turns out it's not very little at all. It's pretty damn hard to do, and you'd be heroic for even trying it.

Want a real spiritual challenge? Want to be a radical follower of Jesus? Want to try something truly heroic? Try the Little Way. Try doing every small thing you do this day with great love. Try waiting in line at the supermarket with great love. Try dealing with an irritating office mate with great love. Try sitting in traffic with great love. Try dealing with your screaming toddler with great love. Try reading your social-media feeds with great love.

Stop trying to be the gifted and talented eye, mouth, hand, or foot of the church, and try for twenty-four hours being the *heart* of the church. Try incarnating the affections of Jesus. Try it and tell me if the Little Way isn't the most heroic and radical thing you've ever attempted in your life.

This is the spiritual genius of Thérèse of Lisieux, the atomic power of the Little Way. She figured out a way to pack radical and heroic discipleship into the nooks and crannies of everyday life. Even the smallest, most ordinary life, like Thérèse's own life, could become the spiritual equivalent of attempting an assault upon Mount Everest. In the hands of Thérèse, "radical" became something anyone could aspire to. Dorothy Day described the Little Way as the "democratization of holiness." You don't need to die a martyr's death or ride off into the sunset like Joan of Arc.

The pursuit of "radical Christianity" is open to everyone.

We do the little things with great love.

12

THE ELEVATOR
TO JESUS

A few years ago, Katy, a student of mine, sought me out for a conversation. She was struggling in a lot of different areas in her life, so we took a walk on our campus. She talked and I listened.

Most of Katy's struggles were with her relationships, so that's most of what we talked about. But late in our walk, our conversation turned to spiritual matters. She shared that she had drifted away from God. She said, "I need to start working on my relationship with God."

And I knew what she meant. She meant what most of us mean when we want to reconnect with God: we need to spend more time in prayer and Bible study, more time with the spiritual disciplines, like fasting. These are the things that we've been taught help us work on our relationship with God.

But I wanted Katy to think about this relationship a bit differently.

"Why," I asked, "would you want to work on your relationship with God?"

Katy looked at me puzzled, "Isn't that what I'm supposed to do?"

"Yes," I said. "But let me ask the question this way: Is there anyone in your life whom you need to apologize to?"

Given everything we'd been talking about, I knew Katy needed to mend some fences. She paused. "Yes," she said.

"Then why don't you give them a call today?" I suggested. "That might be the best way you can work on your relationship with God."

DO THE DISHES FIRST

I was simply quoting the Sermon on the Mount to Katy. To modernize what Jesus says in the sermon, if we are on our way to church and remember that our brother or sister has something against us, we are to turn around and first be reconciled with them. Then we can go to church. That's what I was suggesting to Katy. When we think of "working on our relationship with God," we tend to think about spiritual things that take place between God and ourselves: prayer, Bible study, regular church attendance, fasting, silence, Sabbath. God and me alone together, working our relationship.

When we're "working on our relationship with God," what we don't tend to think about is apologizing to people. We'd much rather pray than apologize. Yet over and over in the Bible, we're told that how we treat people is how we treat God. As it says in 1 John, how can we say we love God, whom we've never seen, while not loving the people we see every day? Jesus comes to us in disguise. When we feel distant from God, we'd like to head to church to work on that relationship. We seek out a praise band rather than a person we've hurt. But the best way to get closer to God, according to Jesus, is to mend our relationships with one another.

We've over-spiritualized our relationship with God, working on a relationship that exists in some unseen, invisible space. We've ignored the social and interpersonal aspects of our relationship with God. As it says in 1 John, anyone who claims to love God but hates a brother or sister is a liar. We are working on our relationship with God when we are working to widen the circle of our affections. Yet, much like Katy, when it comes to getting closer to God, we rarely start with opening our hearts to each other. Think about all the things we do to try to get closer to God and how few of these things move us toward the stranger God. For example, I read a lot of books about Jesus, faith, and theology. I have a huge stack of books on my bedside table. I've spent thousands of dollars and thousands of hours reading books about God and Jesus. But at the end of the day, reading books about Jesus isn't the same as welcoming Jesus in the hungry and the homeless. Maybe you're reading a lot on social media today about Jesus, following the blogs, Facebook, Twitter, and podcast feeds of Christian authors, speakers, and pastors. But spending hours online reading, listening, and writing about Jesus isn't the same as welcoming the Jesus who comes to us in strangers.

The list goes on and on: listening to Christian music, getting a degree in divinity, going to church, lighting candles, attending Christian conferences, jumping up and down at Christian concerts, figuring out your Enneagram number, Bible study, liturgy, *lectio divina*, Bible journaling, contemplative retreats, spiritual direction, listening to sermons on podcasts, improving your theology, decorating your home with Christian stuff, wearing Christian jewelry. These are all good things, all things that could help you get closer to God—but things that, in the final analysis, aren't moving you into the strangeness of welcoming the stranger God.

We can fill our lives full, to overflowing, with things that are good and spiritual but that keep us perpetually distracted from and deferring the work of moving toward each other in love.

On the night before he died, Jesus's last message wasn't a sermon, it was an act of shocking hospitality. Jesus washed his followers' feet and said, "Do this." Hospitality is how we get closer to God.

That's the key—moving toward each other in love. This is precisely the spiritual discipline we so desperately need. We don't need another practice that gets us off alone with God so that God and I can "work on our relationship." We need a spiritual discipline that moves us toward each other in love.

I remember a few years ago I was feeling distant from God, needing to "work on our relationship." To do this, I wanted to become more disciplined in my prayer life. So I was going to use *The Book of Common Prayer* and make the commitment to pray through morning and evening prayers every day. Preparing for this, I was thinking through how I could find quiet time alone with God in the midst of a busy home and work life.

As I was making these plans, I remembered Katy—how moving toward people with love is working on my relationship with God. I looked up and saw our sink full of dirty dishes. And then a thought came unbidden, "Before you starting running off for your alone time with God, do the dishes first."

Spiritual disciplines are great. But let's do the dishes first.

The power of the Little Way, as a spiritual discipline, is that it has you imitating Jesus in your everyday life. The Little Way moves us toward each other in love. The Little Way is a practice that teaches us how to love God through loving people, especially hard-to-love people. As Dorothy Day said, "We love God only as much as the person we love the least." The Little Way teaches us to lean into those places where love is hard, where "heart triggers" abound, where the circle of our affections is pinched and narrowed. That's why the Little Way is described as the science of love, as an education in how to love. Thérèse called the Little Way the elevator to Jesus.

TIME TO PRACTICE!

The third and final manuscript in Thérèse's memoir gives a vision of how she put the Little Way into practice. In the final chapters of *Story of a Soul*, she records everyday examples of the Little Way.[1] Let's

1. Let me say something about my particular approach to the Little

go through two of the most famous examples of the Little Way from *Story of a Soul*.

Like us, Thérèse faced an emotional ecosystem in her convent. Some of the sisters were popular, while others were isolated because they were socially awkward or hard to get along with. Here's how Thérèse described the circles of affection in the convent, the popular sisters contrasted with the shunned:

> *I have noticed (and this is very natural) that the most saintly Sisters are the most loved. We seek their company; we render them services without their asking; finally, these souls so capable of bearing the lack of respect and consideration of others see themselves surrounded with everyone's affection. . . .*

> *On the other hand, imperfect souls are not sought out. No doubt we remain within the limits of religious politeness in their regard, but we generally avoid them, fearing lest we say something which isn't too amiable.*[2]

Way. I describe the Little Way as a practice of hospitality, a social and emotional discipline that widens the circle of our affections. Like any great spiritual master, Thérèse of Lisieux has many expositors and interpreters. Books about the Little Way abound, each with its own perspective. So if you explore the Little Way elsewhere, you'll likely hear it unpacked differently.

The "imperfect souls" have "a lack of judgment, good manners, touchiness in certain characters; all these things which don't make life agreeable." This hasn't changed at all. Think of all the people we try to avoid, all those people who "don't make life agreeable."

As Thérèse looks at the sisters being socially excluded for their difficult personalities, she observes that these social "infirmities" are like a chronic social malady. Sadly, Thérèse concludes, "there is no hope of a cure" for these sisters. Some people are just hard to get along with.

But if these sisters have a chronic social illness, Thérèse makes a startling observation about a mother's love: "I know that my mother would not cease to take care of me, to try to console me, if I remained sick all my life." Notice the affectional work Thérèse is doing: her natural inclination is to lean away from these sisters, but Thérèse pushes herself to adopt a caring, affectional, maternal posture. Maybe these sisters are socially sick, but we take care of the sick. We lean in.

In light of that commitment, Thérèse adopts a practice—a habit-forming discipline—to welcome and embrace the sisters who are being ignored:

2. Thérèse of Lisieux, *Story of a Soul: The Autobiography of Saint Thérèse of Lisieux*, trans. John Clarke, 3rd ed. (Washington, DC: ICS, 1996), 246.

This is the conclusion I draw from this: I must seek
out in recreation, on free days, the company of Sisters
who are the least agreeable to me in order to carry
out with regard to these wounded souls the office of
the Good Samaritan. A word, an amiable smile,
often suffice to make a sad soul bloom.[3]

This is the Little Way as a practice of hospitality, a spiritual discipline of welcome. And the practice here is little, just a kind word or a smile. But the discipline is intentionally seeking out people to deliver the kind word or smile. The practice is to swim against the tide of your feelings, to lean in rather than away, and this widens the circle of our affections by expanding the territory of our kindness. Rather than drifting toward the known and familiar, Thérèse had the Little Way pull her toward a wider group of people.

Further, notice how the *littleness* of what Thérèse did—a kind word or smile to make a sad soul bloom—makes the Little Way something that we practice anytime and anywhere. Sure, we're all busy people. We're stressed, and our schedules are full, so calls to "radical hospitality" can deflate us.

3. Ibid.

When are we going to find the time or energy to do anything radical?

When busy people ask me how they can display "radical hospitality," I tell them to start where Thérèse started. Find someone at work, someone you've ignored, and say hello. Seek them out and offer a kind word and smile. Start there. The Little Way is a practice anyone can do. The power of the Little Way is that it's not trying to fill up your schedule; it's trying to widen your heart.

And most importantly of all, unlike many spiritual disciplines and practices, the Little Way moves us toward the stranger God. The Little Way doesn't pull us away for alone time with God. The Little Way gets us moving toward people with love.

Here's a second example of the Little Way from *Story of a Soul*. Each of us from time to time wakes up on the wrong side of the bed. We find ourselves, for whatever reason, grumpy and irritable. Any little thing sets us off. Someone is talking too loud. The sound of their chewing is grating our nerves. They're sitting too close or going too slow. It doesn't really matter what it is; we're just in a bad mood, and people are driving us crazy.

We know it's just a mood, and it will pass eventually, but in the meantime, we're prickly and mean. We behave and say things we regret. At the very least, we think those dark, antisocial thoughts. We're most definitely not leaning in.

Thérèse had moments just like this; even saints struggle with irritation. So in *Story of a Soul*, she gives another famous example of the Little Way, triggered by a Sister who was making a clicking noise that was driving her crazy at evening prayers:

> For a long time at evening meditation, I was placed in front of a Sister who had a strange habit. . . . As soon as this Sister arrived, she began making a strange little noise which resembled the noise one would make when rubbing two shells, one against the other. . . . It would be impossible for me to tell you how much this little noise wearied me. I had a great desire to turn my head and stare at the culprit who was very certainly unaware of her "click."[4]

It seems like such a small thing, but this is the stuff of life, the annoyances we deal with when living and working with people. We're all tempted to act anti-socially, exactly as Thérèse was, to glare at someone to communicate that they're bothering us. But rather than glare, Thérèse is prompted by the Little Way to target her irritation:

4. Ibid., 249.

I remained calm, therefore, and tried to unite myself to God and to forget the little noise. Everything was useless. I felt the perspiration inundate me. . . .

I searched for a way of [listening to the noise] without annoyance and with peace and joy, at least in the interior of my soul. I tried to love the little noise which was so displeasing; instead of trying not to hear it (impossible), I paid close attention so as to hear it well, as though it were a delightful concert, and my prayer (which was not the Prayer of Quiet) was spent offering this concert to Jesus.[5]

Interpreters of Thérèse often describe the Little Way as a practice of self-mortification, and some of the examples of the Little Way in *Story of a Soul* do have that quality. Thérèse was, after all, a monastic, and there's a bit of that in how she attempts to turn an irritating clicking noise into a "delightful concert" to Jesus. While self-control and self-mastery are important components of the Little Way, interpreting it as a practice of denial and discipline misses the social and affectional focus of the Little Way as the science of love. Thérèse is trying to master and mortify her irritation as she hears the sister's

5. Ibid.

clicking, but the purpose of this mortification, mastering her annoyance, is to widen the circle of her affections to replace irritation with kindness and warmth.

Here's another way to describe this aspect of the Little Way: it's practicing how to wait in a line like Jesus. As we stand in long lines, we grow impatient and irritable; we don't feel particularly warm or affectionate. But the Little Way, as Thérèse shows us, involves widening the circle of our affections while waiting that long checkout line. Ponder the very nature of patience; if it's anything, it's mastering our emotions in order to behave kindly toward others. While self-control is a part of all this, the goal of the discipline is to be social and affectional. Patience isn't merely self-denial; it's a gift of kindness, love, and hospitality.

As a spiritual discipline, there is no indirectness in the Little Way. In practicing the Little Way, we are directly imitating the love of Jesus. And we can do this anytime and anyplace, even standing in that line at the DMV.

This is Thérèse's science of love—small practices that create an elevator to Jesus.

PART IV

PRACTICING HOSPITALITY

13

SEEING

"There goes the terrorist."

Jana had come home upset because of the things people were saying about a new family at the Christian school where she teaches. A husband and wife had just enrolled two beautiful children in the elementary school. The trouble was, they were Muslim.

With their dark skin, accents, and the mom's hijab, the family stood out like a sore thumb here in Abilene, a city in one of the reddest districts in one of the reddest states in America. And their welcome had gotten off to a shaky start. One of the school staff made a comment under her breath when she saw the family dropping off the kids. "There goes the terrorist," she said.

SEEING ABEER

I get it. For a lot of people, a woman in a hijab is one of those emotional triggers we talked about in part 2. You see the hijab, and the circle of your affections shrinks up. The will to embrace evaporates.

A few months later, a graduate student in our psychology program became my thesis student. Abdullah was Muslim; he'd come from Saudi Arabia to study in the United States. In the first weeks that I got to know Abdullah, I found out that he was married and had two young children. "Where do your kids go to school?" I asked. Abdullah told me, and I cringed.

"I know who the terrorist is," I told Jana when I got home that night.

"Really? Who is he?" Jana asked.

"He's Abdullah, my thesis student."

Jana and I pondered the contrast. In the elementary school parking lot, Abdullah was "the terrorist," the scary Muslim man. Across the street at my university, Abdullah was one of our most popular students—warm, gracious, hardworking, and smart. He was one of the best thesis students I've ever had. I loved our year doing research together.

This could have ended up a very sad story about prejudice, but events at Jana's school took a beautiful and surprising turn. There were some unkind whispers when Abdullah's family first showed up, but a few of the young moms at the school saw something different in Abdullah's wife, Abeer. Instead of a Muslim woman in a hijab, they saw a young mother living in a new city far from family and friends. So these West Texas, Republican, evangelical Christian soccer moms invited Abeer and her kids to their weekly playgroup. Unexpected friendships started to grow. When Abdullah finished our program and it was time for his family to return to Saudi Arabia, Abeer and her Christian friends wept because they would miss each other so much.

In a world where there is so much suspicion and prejudice between Christians and Muslims, those soccer moms are heroes of mine. And they provide a beautiful and profound illustration of one of the key practices of the Little Way: seeing.

Seeing is what I find so powerful in the example of the soccer moms at Jana's school. Instead of a hijab, those women saw a lonely young mom. Instead of a Muslim, they saw Abeer.

Social Blindness on
a Brain Scan

In 2006, two neuroscientists from Princeton published research on how certain social emotions affect the brain.[1] Four social emotions were examined: pride, pity, envy, and disgust. American college students looked at pictures of four different sorts of people selected to elicit one of the four social emotions. Pictures of middle-class Americans and American Olympians were selected to elicit the emotion of pride; elderly and disabled people were used to elicit pity; rich businesspeople were used to elicit envy; and homeless persons and drug addicts were used to elicit disgust.

The images triggered their respective emotions, allowing the researchers to watch these emotions on brain scans. The researchers were paying specific attention to a part of the frontal cortex (the medial prefrontal cortex) that's closely associated with social cognition. This part of your brain lights up when you're interacting with a human being, rather than, say, dealing with a rock or a tree.

What the researchers found was disturbing. We'd expect a social center of the brain to light up

1. Lasana T. Harris and Susan T. Fiske, "Dehumanizing the Lowest of the Low," *Psychological Science* 17 (2006): 847–53.

when we're feeling positive social emotions, like pride, looking at people who remind us of ourselves. But what about more negative emotions—emotions like pity or envy? When the subjects of the study looked at pictures of elderly and disabled people or rich businesspeople, they did report feeling pity or envy. Those more negative emotions, thankfully, still triggered the medial prefrontal cortex to light up. Even though the feelings were more negative, the brains of the participants still recognized these people as people.

But things were different for the emotion of disgust, triggered by pictures of homeless persons and drug addicts. When the participants looked at these people, the medial prefrontal cortex didn't light up. The brain was not recognizing the homeless people or the drug addicts as human beings. The brain saw the homeless people and drug addicts not as people, but as *objects*. This is what dehumanization looks like at the neuronal level.

What this brain-imaging research shows us is that we can be looking right at people and not even see them. We can be looking at someone, like a homeless man sleeping on a park bench, and not even see him as a human being.

One of the most common reasons we don't welcome Jesus in disguise is also the simplest: blindness.

Social blindness. We can't see the people standing right in front of us, and it's our emotions that are blinding us.

What that means is that hospitality must begin with seeing people. You can't welcome people when you don't even see them.

THIS IS WATER

So the first practice of the Little Way of hospitality is seeing. Think of how Thérèse practiced seeing in the example from the previous chapter. "I have noticed (and this is very natural) that the most saintly Sisters are the most loved," Thérèse begins. "On the other hand," she continues, "imperfect souls are not sought out . . . we generally avoid them."

"I have noticed." That's where the practice of the Little Way begins, with noticing, with seeing people. Nothing can be accomplished by way of welcoming until we notice others. That's what the soccer moms were able to do with Abeer: they were able to see a lonely young mom in the hijab and thus were able welcome her into their playgroup and, eventually, into their hearts.

Seeing or noticing people is fundamentally a practice of attention. That's how David Foster Wallace describes it in his famous commencement address, "This Is Water."[2] Wallace's remarks are an ode to paying attention, because, as he writes, "it is extremely difficult to stay alert and attentive, instead of getting hypnotized by the constant monologue inside your own head." To illustrate this, Wallace describes the importance of paying attention during "large parts of adult American life that nobody talks about in commencement speeches," the parts of our day that involve "boredom, routine, and petty frustration."

Imagine, Wallace says, finding yourself needing to go to the grocery store after a draining day at work. You're hungry and tired, and all you want to do is go home, but you have to go to the store to get something for dinner. After picking up some food, you're stuck in a long checkout line. Your mood turns black, and you start thinking antisocial thoughts about everyone around you. As Wallace observes, our days are full of these "dreary, annoying, seemingly meaningless routines," from long grocery lines to traffic jams to putting up with annoying people at work.

It's here, Wallace says, in the middle of these annoying and irritating situations, where the

2. Wallace, David Foster, *This Is Water: Some Thoughts, Delivered on a Significant Occasion, about Living a Compassionate Life* (Boston: Little, Brown, 2009).

practice of attention—seeing and noticing the human beings standing right in front of you—is so critical:

> Because my natural default setting is the certainty that situations like this are really all about me . . . and it's going to seem, for all the world, like everybody else is just in my way. . . .

> [But rather than looking at my situation that way,] I can choose to force myself to consider the likelihood that everyone else in the supermarket's checkout line is just as bored and frustrated as I am, and that some of these people actually have much harder, more tedious or painful lives than I do, overall. . . .

> [I]t's hard. It takes will and effort. . . . But if you really learn how to pay attention . . . it will actually be within your power to experience a crowded, hot, slow, consumer-hell-type situation as not only meaningful, but sacred, on fire with the same force that lit the stars: compassion, love, the subsurface unity of all things.[3]

3. David Foster Wallace, "This Is Water," *Alumni Bulletin* (Kenyon College), http://bulletin-archive.kenyon.edu/x4280.html.

Notice how Wallace's example combines everything we've been discussing. Seeing people is a disciplined practice ("It takes will and effort") that widens the circle of our affections, replacing repulsion and contempt ("everybody else is just in my way") with love and compassion.

No One Can Be Mean to You Here

When we see people, we extend kindness to them; we welcome them into our moral circle. Earlier I described the difference between how we treat two different servers at a restaurant—a server who is our friend versus a server who is a stranger. Our friend is inside our moral circle: we see her and extend kindness to her.

Seeing people is a practice of kindness. It was a kind act to invite Abeer to the playgroup. To see someone is to welcome the person into the circle of your affections by giving him or her the gift of kindness. To see someone is to treat the person as kin, as brother or sister and friend. Through kindness, to borrow David Foster Wallace's words, we tap into "the subsurface unity of all things."

I was recently reminded of this practice of the Little Way at an airport. It was late at night when I arrived for the last connecting flight of the day to get back home. The flight kept getting delayed and was eventually canceled. So now it was very late. Everyone on the flight would have to stay the night, coming back the next day to get rebooked on another flight.

For many of us, it had been a very long day, and all we wanted to do was get home. Now we were going to have to stand in a long line to get rebooked, and then off to shuttles to stand in another long line at a hotel to get a room. And then we'd be back the next day to try to get home.

Everyone in that line was hungry, exhausted, and angry—an explosive mixture. And there was only one ticketing agent to rebook all of us. She began slowly working through the line.

As you can imagine, the people in the line didn't treat that ticketing agent with a lot of grace and kindness. Customer after customer treated her roughly and rudely. And I completely understood. I was as upset and as exhausted as everyone else.

The practice of the Little Way is seeing that ticketing agent, to treat her with kindness in the midst of our fatigue and frustration. My wife, Jana, is a master at this, able to insert a kind smile or a joke to set people at ease in tense situations, like that line at the airport.

The kindness we extend to others envelopes them in a space where they are protected from the meanness of the world. It reminds me of a story Jana recently shared with me. A few months ago, one of Jana's students was the first to arrive to her classroom. He walked in, shut the door behind him, and took a long breath. "I've been waiting all day to get to this period," he said. "No one will be mean to me here."

The practice of seeing a ticketing agent in the midst of your fatigue and anger is letting your kindness carve out a space where that agent is protected from the meanness of the world, especially our own meanness.

As Thérèse said, a smile and a kind word often suffice to make a sad soul bloom—or give peace and rest to a traumatized ticketing agent late at night in an airport. In a rough and mean world, our kindness can be an oasis of compassion, holy ground in the midst of anger and scorn.

This is the first practice of the Little Way of hospitality. Seeing, noticing, and extending kindness to the people right in front of us:

The homeless person sleeping on a bench.

The people standing with you in the checkout line.

The airline ticketing agent.

And the Muslim family in your school parking lot.

14

STOPPING

In 1970, psychologists John Darley and Daniel Batson decided to replicate Jesus's most famous parable,
the Good Samaritan. Where Jesus had ancient Jewish clergy, a priest and a Levite, passing by the man
beaten on the side of the road, Darley and Batson
studied the helpfulness of seminarians preparing for
the ministry at Princeton Theological Seminary.[1]

They set up the experiment outside. The seminarians were coordinated to pass a person slumped
in a doorway, and when they passed, the person in
the doorway would let out a painful groan, as if in
physical distress and pain, possibly requiring medical attention. As the seminarians passed the man,
the psychologists took note of a simple variable: who

1. J. M. Darley and C. D. Batson, "From Jerusalem to Jericho: A Study of
Situational and Dispositional Variables in Helping Behavior," *Journal
of Personality and Social Psychology* 27 (1973): 100–108.

stopped to ask if the man in the doorway was okay. Would these seminarians, like the priest and Levite in the parable of the Good Samaritan, pass by on the other side of the road?

That was the basic idea, but Darley and Batson added two interesting twists to the classic story.

First, before being sent out to pass by the groaning man in the doorway, the seminarians were told they were going to give a brief talk at a different location (a location that would cause them to pass the groaning man). The subject of the brief talk varied. Half of them were to read and then share reflections about, you guessed it, the parable of the Good Samaritan. The other half read and were to talk about a topic unrelated to helping people. So that was the first twist.

The second twist was time pressure. As the seminarians were sent to the next location, they were put under time pressure. Seminarians in the "low hurry" group were told they had plenty of time to get to the location of their talk. In fact, they'd likely have to wait once they got there. Seminarians in the "high hurry" condition were told they were already late for the talk, people were waiting on them, and "you'd better hurry."

With these two additional twists, these future leaders of the church were sent out to pass by a man in need of help. And the psychologists were watching.

So who would stop to help? There were three possible hypotheses. First, maybe almost everyone would stop to help.

Or maybe help would be prompted by what the seminarians had on their minds. That was the second hypothesis. Maybe if you're thinking about the parable of the Good Samaritan, you'll be better able to spot similar situations in your own life. That seems to be the basic idea behind sermons and Bible classes—that if you are taught the parable of the Good Samaritan, you'll be more likely to act like the Good Samaritan in your own life.

Or maybe it's all about having the time to help. That was the third hypothesis. Maybe we're more likely to help when we have the time. Maybe the priest and Levite in the parable in the Good Samaritan passed by because they were in a hurry.

The results of the experiment were clear. Only one variable predicted who would stop: time. The seminarians most likely to stop were those who had the time.

THE SPEED OF LOVE

One of the reasons we don't see each other, why we pass by each other on the road, is the pace of our lives. We hurt and wound each other with our hurry. The speed at which we move through our days is a form of violence.

Seeing each other requires that we become interruptible. So that's another key practice of the Little Way of hospitality. We practice hospitality when we practice *interruptibility*. Seeing requires stopping.

We describe hospitality as "making room," and we tend to think of this as making room in physical space—making room at our table or making a bed available in our home. The practice of stopping is a different sort of making room. Interruptibility is a practice of making room in *time*, finding space for others in the midst of our busy day. That's the inhospitality of hurry; there's no room for you in my schedule.

We can make ourselves more interruptible and available to each other by addressing the inhospitable pace of our lives. Kosuke Koyama suggests that slowness is the pace of God's love: "Love has its speed. It is an inner speed. It is a spiritual speed. It is a different kind of speed from the technological speed to which we are accustomed. It is 'slow' yet it is lord over all other speeds since it is the speed of love."[2] Slowing down is a practice of hospitality because it makes us available to each other.

Still, even if we can slow the pace of our lives, there will be interruptions. Hurry is a part of life, and that hurry narrows the circle of our affections. We become abrupt, curt, and rude, or we simply blow past the people who need us in that moment.

When we stop, we must practice being present and available. For me, this often means turning and squarely facing the person. Too often, when I stop, I still have one foot out the door. Physically, I'm leaning away rather than in. And I'm often only paying partial attention, my mind racing ahead of my body. Like my body, I'm emotionally leaning away. Stopping involves slowing down that mental hurry, relaxing the body, and being fully present to each other, physically and mentally. Again, these are little practices and disciplines: facing people, staying relaxed, being present, working hard to listen. These are practices of hospitality that widen the circle of our affections—practices that we can work on anytime and anywhere.

Stopping, as a practice of the Little Way of hospitality, is the practice of seeing people in the midst

2. Philip D. Kenneson, *Life on the Vine: Cultivating the Fruit of the Spirit in Christian Community* (Downers Grove, IL: InterVarsity, 1999), 124.

of our hurry. Think about how Jesus noticed and stopped for people when he traveled:

> *Then they came to Jericho. As Jesus and his disciples, together with a large crowd, were leaving the city, a blind man, Bartimaeus (which means "son of Timaeus"), was sitting by the roadside begging. When he heard that it was Jesus of Nazareth, he began to shout, "Jesus, Son of David, have mercy on me!"*
>
> *Many rebuked him and told him to be quiet, but he shouted all the more, "Son of David, have mercy on me!"*
>
> *Jesus stopped.* (Mark 10:46–49a)

I think our Christian witness hangs on those two words: *Jesus stopped.*

The Good Samaritan stopped. Jesus stopped. Will we stop?

What Darley and Batson's study with hurried seminarians tells us is that most of us are Jesus hobbyists. We pursue our hobbies when we have free and spare time. And that's how we treat Jesus. We'll welcome people like the Good Samaritan when we have the time. We get around to Jesus after all the other important stuff on our To Do list has been checked off. We follow Jesus if we're available, which means following Jesus has become a hobby.

The practice of stopping, the discipline of being interruptible, is what turns a hobbyist into a follower of Jesus.

Because it's often inconvenient, stopping requires discipline. But it's a discipline that allows Jesus to come to us in disguise. We instinctively associate Jesus with the Good Samaritan in his parable, but many interpreters think the deeper insight is to identify Jesus with the man beaten on the side of the road: Jesus in disguise again, just as he is in Matthew 25. Stopping, even when its painfully inconvenient, allows us to welcome Jesus into our lives.

On my blog, I wrote about the Darley and Batson study, and a reader shared this story:[3]

> *I heard of this study many years ago and was just telling a friend about it yesterday. I was reminded of it when I headed out in a snowstorm for my graduate class on death, dying and bereavement on*

3. Julie, comment in response to Richard Beck, "A Jesus Hobbyist," *Experimental Theology* (blog), January 21, 2016, http://experimentaltheology.blogspot.com/2016/01/a-jesus-hobbyist.html#comment-2473693926.

Monday. My neighbor, an elderly Cambodian man with schizophrenia and terminal cancer, was walking to the bank and asked if he could accompany me.

I knew it would make me late for class and keep me out longer in the storm, but I also realized that it was a good thing to do. We had a lovely chat and he sweetly bowed to me as we parted. I was late for class.

The next day he died of a heart attack while receiving his chemotherapy treatment.

I am grateful for our walk together.

Jesus will make you late. But he comes to us, even in the middle of snowstorms.

15

APPROACHING

It was 8:00 p.m., evening medication time. I walked into the Highland Assisted Living facility to find all the residents standing in a long line, waiting to get their evening meds. Highland serves people who have of cognitive disabilities or psychiatric issues and cannot live independently, but they do well in a semi-structured environment.

I know everyone at Highland, so the entire line greeted me happily. They know I'm there to visit Kristi, but since I've formed relationships with many of the residents, I spend some time catching up on the news.

I've been coming to Highland to see Kristi and take her shopping for a couple of years now. And that night, as I stood in line talking with everyone, I mused about how these unlikely friendships of mine came about. Whenever I talk to audiences about hospitality, the question always gets asked, "Where do we start? What is one practical thing we can do to become more hospitable?" I answer by introducing the Little Way, explaining how Thérèse would seek out the sisters in her convent who, for whatever reason, were being ignored or excluded.

"So start there," I answer. "Pick someone in your life—someone at work or at church. Go up to them and offer a kind word and smile."

It's really as simple as that. Pick someone and make contact, just as Thérèse did. That was her practice of the Little Way: "I must seek out." We can call this practice *approaching*.

That's how all my relationships at the Highland Assisted Living facility got started. Having learned about the Little Way and Thérèse's practice of seeking out and intentionally approaching people on the social margins, I began to adopt this practice. One Sunday, I stood in the middle of my church and looked around. I asked myself, "Who is someone I normally wouldn't speak to? Who am I not seeing?"

I scanned the room and saw Kristi, wearing big sunglasses because of her blindness, sitting in a wheelchair along the back wall of the church. I don't have huge emotional triggers about disabilities, but I knew that, if left to my own devices, I probably wouldn't go up and introduce myself to the blind stranger in the wheelchair. Left to my own devices, I would do what I always did at church—look for someone I knew, a friend, and catch up with them.

But that particular Sunday, in my first attempt to practice the Little Way, I sought out Kristi. I approached and introduced myself. "Hello, my name is Richard." And that's how it all started: with a simple hello.

I kept seeking out Kristi every Sunday. As I've shared, eventually Kristi started sitting with my family during services. Soon after that, Kristi started coming to our adult Bible class, where she formed a whole other set of friends, most of them the team of women who wheel her to the restroom. During the week, I started visiting Kristi at Highland to chat or take her shopping. And over the years of visiting Kristi, I've gotten to know all the other residents at Highland, forming even more friendships. A whole other world of friendships opened up to me. Today, I spend less time with middle-class folk and people with PhDs and more time with inmates and people with cognitive disabilities. My friendship group has been flipped on its head, all because I approached a stranger in a wheelchair to say hello. Yes, it seems like such a little thing, this practice of approaching, but the Little Way changed my life.

NO MORE DETOURS

A critical aspect of the practice of approaching is intentionally going against the grain of your emotional and social triggers. The practice of approaching is habitually leaning in where your default is to lean away, the way those Texas soccer moms leaned in when they saw a woman in a hijab. That day when I said hello to Kristi, there was enough about her appearance—the blindness, the wheelchair—to create some awkwardness. I wasn't repulsed or repelled, but I most definitely wasn't drawn to Kristi. I was, ever so slightly, leaning away.

The practice of approaching is intentionally reversing this trend, going against the tide of our emotions to widen the circle of our affections. My favorite example of this in *Story of a Soul* is Thérèse's reflections on the Little Way of loving our enemies.

Jesus taught us to love our enemies. But if our lives are like Thérèse's, we don't have a ton of enemies, people malevolently seeking our doom. We are, though, surrounded by people we'd rather avoid. As Thérèse describes it, "No doubt, we don't have any enemies in Carmel, but there are feelings. One feels attracted to this Sister, whereas with regard to another, one would make a long detour in order to avoid meeting her. And so, without knowing it, she becomes the subject of persecution. Well, Jesus is telling me that it is this Sister who must be loved."[1]

I just love Thérèse's assessment. We don't have many enemies, but there are feelings! My friend Randy Harris says we don't have enemies in our lives as much as we have irritants. Think about the workplace or even church; think about all the feelings going on. I like her. I'm jealous of him. I have a grudge here, some resentment there. I feel annoyance, irritation, scorn, contempt. He's weird; she's a freak show. Our social world is an ecosystem of emotions, a zoo of feelings.

Those feelings narrow the circle of our affections and the territory of our kindness. Thérèse's example of this is very on point. How many times have you taken a detour around someone when you've seen that person coming? I ask audiences to raise their hands if they've ever detoured around people at church. The whole room raises their hands.

The practice of approaching, as Thérèse describes it, is going against our desire to detour. All the feelings in our social world cause people to be ignored, isolated, and marginalized. People are detoured around, and Thérèse describes this as a form of social persecution. The practice of

1. Thérèse of Lisieux. *Story of a Soul: The Autobiography of Saint Thérèse of Lisieux*, trans. John Clarke, 3rd ed. (Washington, DC: ICS, 1996), 225.

approaching breaks up these bubbles of isolation, moving us toward people while others are moving away.

DISENGAGE THE SOCIAL AUTOPILOT

The sad thing is that a lot of this detouring and ignoring is happening unconsciously. We're not intentionally trying to be mean or unkind or cliquish. Our feelings just naturally pull us in these directions, away from each other. We're on social autopilot, and that autopilot follows the path of least resistance. Remember how I described the instinct to look for your friends as our number-one hospitality problem? That's the social autopilot at work. No one is being wicked when looking for their friends, but that automatic instinct narrows the circle of our affections, causing us to detour around people.

So the practice of approaching is disengaging the social autopilot and taking over the controls to move toward people we wouldn't otherwise welcome.

When you're on social autopilot, it doesn't take much to cause you to lean away from people. A little bit of feeling, the slightest twinge of awkwardness, can have a huge social impact—the difference between talking to someone or not. The practice of approaching is to move into that awkwardness, into the strangeness. When you are disciplined about this, what you find is that the awkwardness slowly disappears and is replaced by affection and love. You welcome the stranger God.

Before I knew Kristi, I felt a wee bit awkward around people with disabilities and wheelchairs. But now that I know Kristi, my affections have exploded. Today, the very first people I look for and am drawn to in any social situation are people with disabilities and wheelchairs. My affection for Kristi has blown my heart wide open.

Once again, Jesus came to me in disguise.

It's two weeks before Christmas as I write this. Last night at church, I was visiting with Kristi, and she asked me to help her hand out her Christmas cards. Since Kristi is blind, she can't see the names written on her cards, cards someone at Highland helped her write. So I read the name aloud on each card, handed it to Kristi and then went looking for that person, telling the recipient that Kristi had a Christmas card for him or her. One by one, people came over to Kristi to receive their card—each moment holy and sacred. And I got to witness and be a part of it all. Finally, there was one card left, and I read my name. Unbidden, tears came to my eyes.

It's strange, how grace finds you in these little

things. Love and joy have a way of sneaking up and surprising you.

I read my Christmas card that was signed, "Love, Kristi."

We hugged, wished each other a Merry Christmas, and made our plans to see each other the next day.

Christmas was around the corner, and we both, my friend and I, had more Christmas shopping to do.

PART V

HOW TO SAVE
THE WORLD

16

LOVE LOCALLY

The motto of my university is "Change the World." A lot of us want to change the world. At the very least, we want to make a positive difference.

So it's not all that surprising that when I speak to audiences about the Little Way—breaking it down in the practices of seeing, stopping, and approaching—some people are less than impressed. "That's it?" they ask. "Just smile at people and say hi? The world is falling apart; big changes have to be made. And all you are recommending is friendly greetings and kind words?"

Don't Knock It until You Try It

There is a littleness to the Little Way that can be offensive, especially given all the problems the world is facing. That was the reaction Dorothy Day had upon first encountering the Little Way. She considered the Little Way too small to make any meaningful impact. We want to be heroes, and the Little Way doesn't seem very heroic.

My response to this criticism of the Little Way is simple: Try it. Live into the practices of seeing, stopping, and approaching, and then get back to me. You'll discover that the Little Way is pretty damn heroic. It is one of the most difficult and challenging spiritual-formation practices you'll ever encounter.

That's exactly what changed the mind of Dorothy Day. Day, like Thérèse, had heroic aspirations, and you'd be hard-pressed to find a Christian witness as radical as hers. For instance, Day was jailed many times because of her protests, the last time when she was seventy-five years old! If you're getting thrown in jail as a senior citizen, you're pretty hard-core. And beyond her activism, Dorothy Day lived in voluntary poverty, sharing life with and extending hospitality to the poor and homeless. By any measure, Dorothy Day was a radical Christian. But even Dorothy Day, the radical political activist, came to see herself as a follower of the Little Way. So did Mother Teresa of Calcutta.

So don't criticize the Little Way as little until you try it. If you follow the path of the Little Way, little by little, you will find yourself living in a more "radical" lifestyle. It won't feel radical at first, as I found out the first time I said hello to Kristi, but time passes, and suddenly you notice you are spending your days at an assisted-living facility or in a prison. That's what happened to me. Drop by drop, the Little Way adds up to something huge.

BEYOND FEELINGS

But let's also situate the practice of the Little Way within a larger vision of the kingdom of God. I want to show you how the Little Way can save the world.

The end game with the Little Way isn't emotional; it's about breaking down affectional barriers so that surprising and unexpected friendships can happen—like what happened with Daryl Davis and the former Klansmen, Jana and Ruthie, and Kristi and me.

So we need to make a distinction between the Little Way and a broad call for universal compassion and empathy. When we speak about "widening the circle of our affections," we are talking about the *intentional and disciplined practice* of seeing, stopping for, and approaching people whom we otherwise would avoid or ignore. "Widening the circle of our affections" is not describing a generic love for the world. That's because compassion and empathy have a dark side, and the Little Way protects us from these temptations.

"While we are alone, we could believe we loved everyone."[1] That's my favorite quote from Jean Vanier, the founder of the L'Arche Community, where people with and without intellectual disabilities live and work together as peers to create inclusive communities of faith and friendship, communities that transform society through these relationships that cross social boundaries. There is perhaps no better example of the Little Way in practice than the day-to-day life in a L'Arche community, where little things—like cooking, cleaning, and bathing—are done with great love.

Vanier's point in his quote is that when we love people generically and abstractly, we can trick ourselves into believing that we love everyone in the entire world. We always imagine ourselves to be kind and compassionate people, that our affections embrace all of humanity.

Social media enhances this illusion. Every day our social-media feeds expose us to the suffering of the world, from war atrocities, to shootings, to refugee crises, to homelessness, to poverty, to abuse, to human trafficking. The hearts of compassionate

---

1. Jean Vanier, *Community and Growth* (New York: Paulist, 1991), 26.

people ache with the news of every tragedy. Through social media, the circle of our affections seems to widen in an embrace of the entire world. Our big hearts absorb it all.

But there are some problems with social-media compassion. First of all, compassion is a stress reaction, which can lead to what psychologists call empathy or compassion fatigue. The word *compassion* literally means "suffering with." These sympathetic feelings affect us, physically and emotionally. As we watch our social-media feeds, scrolling through tragedy after tragedy, the stress response mounts. We grow increasingly agitated, upset, and distressed. We become exhausted and depleted, leading to emotional and physical breakdowns. It's impossible for one heart to carry the suffering of the entire world, and it's impossible for one person to mend all that is broken in the world. So our stress is compounded with a sense of futility, despair, and hopelessness. It's all too big for us to fix. In short, our empathy for everyone in the world makes us anxious and upset, leading to depression, despair and cynicism. Eventually, we burn out.

Compassion, for it to find a healthy and sustainable outlet, needs to find a more personal, more intimate scale of action. Compassion works best face-to-face. When we care for each other face-to-face, the stress reaction is matched by the intimacy, warmth, connection, and solidarity we feel in each other's presence—two souls reaching out and making contact. That's the spiritual genius of a L'Arche community—how it roots compassion in face-to-face relationships. Social media doesn't allow us to make these intimate life-giving connections. All our social-media feeds produce is a one-sided sympathetic stress reaction, day after day. Over time, we either burn out or go numb.

In contrast to social media, the arena of action of the Little Way is the intimate and personal. Practicing the Little Way isn't a generic call for more compassion. Instead, it brings you into contact with actual people. The Little Way is practiced face-to-face. We welcome the Jesus who comes to us in disguise—the person physically standing right in front of us.

This is not to say that we don't love everyone in the entire world or feel compassion for everyone we see on our social-media feed. It's just the simple truth that we love the whole world best by loving the piece of it right in front of us. There's a famous saying for environmental activism, "Think globally, act locally." The Little Way is the social version of this. A motto for the Little Way would be "Care globally, love locally."

The other reason we love locally is that the concrete acts of caring for each other are where compassion is translated into care. Compassion is a vital first step, but compassion isn't care, and perhaps most importantly, compassion isn't a relationship or a friendship.

Far too many of us love issues more than human beings. When we're alone on social media, we trick ourselves into thinking that we love everyone. This happens because we love and care about all the right *issues*. For example, I have many Christian friends who care enormously about the issue of homelessness. Yet few of these friends actually know a homeless person or have welcomed a homeless person into their own home. It's so much easier to have compassion for the homeless in the abstract, as an issue, than to actually approach a homeless person to enter into a surprising friendship. This is the unique and particular power of the Little Way—how through practices like seeing, stopping, and approaching, you are drawn into relationships with actual people. The Little Way isn't a bland call to become more compassionate. The Little Way is a catalyst for welcoming people face-to-face.

The trouble with thinking that we love everyone is that it blinds us to how narrow our love actually is. We love everyone until I mention who I voted for in the last election, or smell so bad you have to plug your nose, or any of the other emotional triggers we surveyed. No one loves everyone. We have issues with people. As Thérèse said, there are feelings.

The potency of the Little Way is that it forces you to admit and face the ways in which you push people away. The Little Way forces you to confront your failures of love by practicing moving toward those you find hard to love. The Little Way doesn't let you off the hook with generic, feel-good calls for more love and compassion. The Little Way has you learning to love the hard-to-love person standing right in front of you. The Little Way isn't sappy emotionalism; it's a discipline and training in how to love, especially where it's hard to love. Because that's where the rubber meets the road. As Dorothy Day put it, "We love God only as much as the person we love the least." That's the hard, heroic road of the Little Way. That's the elevator to Jesus.

CONTACT BREEDS COMPASSION

But the Little Way isn't just disciplined spiritual practice; it's also good science. Our social biases and prejudices make it difficult to overcome problems like racism. Heroic, change-the-world activists have to face the fact that you can't change prejudices through better policy or law.

For example, in the wake of the police shootings that roiled America and gave rise to the Black Lives Matter movement, I took a bus trip with twenty preachers from my faith tradition. There were ten white preachers and ten black, and we discussed what our churches could do to help overcome our racial divisions. During the trip, we had the privilege to spend time with Fred Gray, the famous civil-rights attorney who was the lawyer for Rosa Parks and Martin Luther King Jr. during the Montgomery bus boycott. Outside of Thurgood Marshall, Fred Gray is the most significant civil-rights lawyer in American history, the lawyer who filed seminal school integration lawsuits and who represented the victims of the infamous Tuskegee syphilis study. During our time with Fred Gray, we asked him about why we've experienced so little racial progress since in the 1960s. "I was able to change the laws," he said, "but I couldn't change the hearts."

Changing hearts, as a science of love, is the focus of the Little Way, and the research about how you change prejudice is clear. It happens through inter-personal contact, specifically face-to-face contact, where we interact with each other as equals.

The trouble is, because we move though the

world on emotional autopilot, our biases and prejudices lead us away from people, creating distance. Contact doesn't happen. This creates a perverse negative feedback loop. Unconscious bias causes us to lean away from people, which reduces contact and leaves our bias intact. Rinse and repeat.

The genius of the Little Way, especially in its practice of approaching, is that it is a spiritual discipline that produces contact. We practice leaning in where we had been leaning away. And this practice, because it produces interpersonal contact, is scientifically proven to change hearts. We combat emotional biases like racism not by passing laws or policy, but by loving locally.

And this goes for any prejudice or bias we may have. The power of the Little Way is that it asks us to inventory our hearts to identify our biases and prejudices, all the emotional triggers that cause us to hesitate in welcoming each other, and then to intentionally approach. You make contact. Yes, this contact might seem small and ineffective at first—just a smile and a kind word. But repeated contact eventually widens the circle of our affections, for any and all of our biases and prejudices.

ATOMIC POWER

The Little Way might seem little, but it's a revolutionary tool of social change. It's really pretty simple. If interpersonal contact is the only way to overcome bias and prejudice, then you have to be disciplined and intentional in making that contact. You have to move against the grain of your emotional triggers. You have to take the controls away from your social autopilot.

The "atomic power" of the Little Way is that it changes the world through little things. I like the assessment of the American psychologist and philosopher William James: "I am against bigness and greatness in all their forms; and with the invisible molecular moral forces that work from individual to individual, stealing through the crannies of this world like so many soft rootlets, or like the capillary oozing of water and yet rending the hardest monuments of man's pride, if you give them time."[2]

This is how the world changes—through the "moral forces that work from individual to individual." But this change doesn't happen automatically.

2. From a letter to Mrs. Henry Whitman from William James dated June 7, 1899. Robert Dale Richardson, *William James in the Maelstrom of American Modernism: A Biography* (Boston: Houghton Mifflin, 2007), 384.

It requires discipline and intentionality; it requires getting out of your comfort zone; it requires facing up to and moving against ingrained biases and prejudices. It requires seeing, stopping, and approaching. This is the change that follows when we take up the practices of the Little Way, caring for the entire world but learning to love locally.

17

BLEST BE THE (WEAK) TIE THAT BINDS

"Please pray that I get some teeth."

Week after week, this was Beth's prayer request at Freedom's Tuesday-night ladies' Bible class. Lacking access to a dental plan, Beth had lost all her teeth over the years. The only dental attention a lot of our poor and homeless friends at Freedom get is pulling bad teeth. Just the other day, while visiting the gang at Highland Assisted Living, my friend Paul informed me that he's now down to his last tooth. I made sure the Christmas cookies I got for Paul this year were soft.

Beth worked in home health care, and she was really good at her job. But without teeth, it was hard for Beth to get a job. Without teeth, your smile is compromised. Without teeth, you look older and more sinister—and poor. Not having teeth is one of those social triggers, changing your appearance just enough to cause people to hesitate and lean away, just enough that the job goes to someone else.

So week after week, during the prayer request time at the ladies' Bible class, Beth asked the women to pray that she get some teeth. How Beth's prayers were answered is a wonderful illustration of how the Little Way can save the world.

THE MOST IMPORTANT WORD IN THE BIBLE

The theologian Samuel Wells says that the most important word in the Bible is *with*.[1] But the word we tend to focus on is *for*. Because we are caring and compassionate people, we like to do things *for* people. Our cities and churches are filled with all sorts of programs that do things *for* people. We can work at a food pantry. We can volunteer for a job-training program, a school mentoring program, or a Christmas toy drive. We can send money to nonprofits

---

1. Samuel Wells, *A Nazareth Manifesto* (Chichester: Wiley-Blackwell, 2015).

doing good work around the world. We can donate, give, and serve in a million different ways.

Wells points out that we like to do things for people because we want to fix things. The world seems awfully broken and messed up, and we'd like to help. So we roll up our sleeves and get to work, working hard for hurting people. *For* also makes us feel good. It's the hero's role. Working for people makes us feel useful, as if we're making a difference and changing the world.

Working for people, serving and caring for people, is valuable and necessary work. But as you've likely noticed, *working for* people rarely translates into *being with* people. All those service projects and volunteer hours—working for people—rarely translate into relationships and friendships.

Every Thanksgiving in my town, there's a huge meal that's provided in the Civic Center for hundreds of poor and homeless people, people who would not have otherwise had a big turkey-and-dressing meal. Dozens and dozens of volunteers work this event. Thousands of dollars are donated for the food and the space. The local news covers the event. Community nonprofits and churches show pictures of the meal, and all the volunteers feel grateful for being a part of something important and meaningful.

But how many friendships get formed from this Thanksgiving meal? How many ongoing and lasting relationships?

Our community Thanksgiving meal is a classic example of working *for* people. Dozens of people slaving in the kitchen, serving the food line, refilling drinks, cleaning it all up—the whole meal is an explosion of kind, charitable activity. All hands are on deck to serve a meal for the poor and homeless.

But what about being *with* the poor and homeless? What about intimacy and friendship?

Wells points out that what most of us really want in life isn't people doing things *for* us. We don't want to be fixed. We don't want to be someone else's service project. What we all deeply crave is community, belonging, intimacy, connection, and friendship. We want *with* rather than *for*.

The Little Way seems little, unheroic, and inconsequential to us because the Little Way specializes in *with* rather than *for*. The Little Way isn't aimed at fixing people's problems, working for them. The discipline of the Little Way is being with, widening the circle of our affections to open our hearts to surprising, unexpected friendships.

The practices of the Little Way—seeing, stopping, and approaching—don't try to fix people; they make us available to each other. True, approaching people with some kind words and conversation doesn't seem like a strategy that can solve poverty and homelessness. But these kind words and conversation—being with, rather than working for—break down social and emotional barriers that pave the way for intimacy, relationship, and friendship.

THE STRENGTH OF WEAK TIES

Yet before we think friendship is useless as a tool for helping fix problems in the world, let's take a lesson from the early church and from sociological research. Maybe the Little Way, with simple things like crossing a room to say hello, can save the world after all.

Let's start with the early Christians. Ponder a curious fact about the witness of the early Christians in light of our tendency to focus on electoral politics as the weapon of choice to "change the world." Following the example of Jesus, the early Christians ignored the state. Instead, they extended care and aid to those in their community who were destitute and in need. The early Christians sold their land and possessions, sharing them with each other so that "there were no needy persons among them" (Acts 2:42–47; 4:32–37). Problems like hunger and homelessness were dealt with in the intimate sphere of friendship, the community of Jesus followers who were of "one heart and mind."

In Acts 2, the Greek word *koinonia* is used to describe this "at-oneness" among the early Christians. *Koinonia* describes community, intimacy, sharing, gift-giving and friendship. *Koinonia* is how the early Christians understood Jesus's claim that "the kingdom of God is in your midst." *Koinonia* was how the confession "Jesus is Lord" was made real and enjoyed. *Koinonia* is how the early Christians made the kingdom of God come on earth as it is in heaven.

This was (and remains) a hard labor, emotionally and relationally. The early Christians struggled with the same racial and socioeconomic biases that we struggle with today. They leaned away from each other the same way we lean away from each other. Yes, the early Christians cared for each other, but not always. Like us, they had their prejudices. But notice, again, where those prejudices were called out, confronted, and dealt with. Prejudices and discrimination were handled face-to-face in the intimate community of fellow believers. Paul's revolutionary declaration—"There is no longer Jew or Gentile, slave or free, male and female" (Galatians 3:28)—had to get worked out face-to-face. It was a fragile business, this awkward and difficult work to build bridges between people. And the practices of the Little Way—seeing, stopping for, and approaching each other in love—would have been the first steps in bringing about the social revolution that Paul announced.

Yes, the world is facing huge problems, from poverty to homelessness to prejudice to discrimination. But the early Christians didn't turn to the state for answers and solutions. They turned toward each other. They fought the battles being waged in their hearts. The early Christians practiced a radical, local politics of care so that there was no needy person among them. The church cared globally but loved locally. The early followers of Jesus created revolutionary social communities where demographic and economic barriers were torn down. And the tool that ignited and sustained this revolution, where the marginalized, downtrodden, and destitute flocked to the fellowship of the early Christians, was *koinonia*. The first followers of Jesus changed the world through friendship.

Still, there's something in us that doesn't quite believe this, so let me offer an explanation that sociologists have given to show how all this works. Plus, I'll tell you the story of how Beth got some new teeth.

One of the biggest factors associated with poverty in America is *concentrated* poverty. We call the places where this exists slums, ghettos, trailer parks, or projects—places where everyone who lives there is poor. Studies have shown that people who live in areas of concentrated poverty have difficulty escaping poverty. Poor families have better prospects if they live in a more diverse neighborhood, with middle-class neighbors around them. Neighbors matter.

One of the reasons has to do with what sociologists call *social capital*, the depth and breadth of your social connections. When you have connections and friendships with many and diverse sorts of people, you have a lot of social capital; you are socially "rich." You might even describe yourself as a networker, someone who knows lots of people and who likes getting people connected. I have a friend like this, and he is always saying things like this to me: "You don't know Jim? How can that be? I have to get you two together!" My friend has a lot of social capital. He seems to know everyone, and he's always introducing people to each other. By contrast, if you have just a few friends, and all your friends are very similar to you, then you have little social capital. You would be socially "poor."

Material poverty, studies tell us, is associated with low social capital. The poor lack wide and diverse friendships. This explains why concentrated poverty is so toxic and why neighbors matter. Concentrated poverty reduces social capital, depriving the poor of acquaintances, contacts, networks, and friendships that can help lift them out of poverty.

In 1973, the sociologist Mark Granovetter published a study entitled "The Strength of Weak Ties."[2] In Granovetter's terminology, a "strong tie" is a strong, intimate relationship, like a very close friend. A "weak tie," by contrast, is an acquaintance, someone you know on a first-name basis but not very well.

Granovetter studied how people looked for a good job—something, obviously, that would be of interest to people trying to climb out of poverty. What he found was that people tended to find new jobs through their weak-tie relationships rather than their strong ties. Simply put, when a person is looking for a new job, acquaintances are often more helpful than friends.

Why is that? Because friends, our strong ties, tend to move in the same, small social world in which we move. While these friends are vital in helping us feel connected, loved, and known, this intimate circle of friends has only limited connections with the outside world. Our friendships are

2. Mark S. Granovetter, "The Strength of Weak Ties," *American Journal of Sociology* 78 (1973): 1360–80.

deep, but they often aren't wide. Because like is attracted to like, friendships support us but don't generally connect us with diverse sorts of people. Friends tend to cluster in clumps of sameness, limiting their ability to help us make connections with different sorts of people.

And making connections with a wide, diverse set of people, it turns out, is exactly what you need when searching for a job. This is the "strength" of the weak tie. The strong ties, our friends, provide us with love and intimacy; our weak ties, our acquaintances, provide us with breadth, with a network that connects us far and wide.

In Granovetter's study, that's how people found their new jobs—not through their strong ties, but through their weak ones. For example, you have a friend whose brother works with a big company, so you give him a call. Your friend is a strong tie, but his brother is a weak one; you've only met him once before. But that weak tie helps you find out about the job prospects in the company, something your friend cannot help with. This illustrates the power of the weak tie. Strong ties provide us with support, but weak ties help us search.

As another example, think about a time when you've moved to a new town. Think about how your friends and family pointed you to weak ties in the new town. "Look up my cousin," they encourage you. Or perhaps you have your own weak tie in that town, an old college friend you haven't seen in years. You look her up on Facebook to reconnect. Over coffee or through Facebook, that old acquaintance gives you advice about neighborhoods to move to, good schools, and job prospects.

This is the power of a rich social network—its mixture of deep and wide relationships. And this is what gets undermined by concentrated poverty. In concentrated poverty, people are cut off from the rich and diverse networks of friends, acquaintances, and neighbors we need to navigate life and solve our problems.

Just think about how vital your social connections are in helping you face and overcome the obstacles in your own life. Most of us cannot see our social network at work, taking for granted its invisible, life-supporting existence, as we do with the air we breathe. So consider a day in the life of a middle-class social network:

Your baby has a strange cough. So you call your friend who is a nurse to ask her some questions.

Your computer crashes, so you call your acquaintance who is an Apple wizard. He tells you how to push some strange configuration of keyboard controls, and your computer comes back to life.

Your car is making a strange noise. So you ask your neighbor, who is a mechanic, to listen to it. He spots the problem, saving you hundreds of dollars.

You'd like to take out a loan to do some home improvements. So you approach the class member in your Bible class who works for a bank, to get some guidance.

A plumbing issue comes up in your house, and you ask friends on Facebook for recommendations of trustworthy plumbers in town.

These are not hypotheticals. Jana and I have done each of these things. And it's likely that you have, too. These appeals to our social support network are so normal and natural that we don't ever notice how vital they are in solving the problems of life.

The only time you notice your social safety net is when it goes away. The easiest way for some of us to recall what this feels like is to remember a time when we moved to a new city and knew absolutely no one. And then something bad happened—a computer crashed or our car broke down. There's absolutely no one around who you can call to get some help—no one to help, answer a question, drive you around, or point you in the right direction. You're 100 percent alone.

At some point in our lives, we've all felt this—

what it's like to be left without a social support network. You've felt it when a crisis strikes when traveling abroad or after moving to a new town. We take our social network for granted, only noticing how vital it is once it's gone. Suddenly we realize we can't live without it.

That brings us back to our desire to do things *for* the poor. The truth of the matter is that "the poor" are capable and resourceful. What the poor lack isn't competency but connection. The poor are very much able to overcome the problems they face; they just need to be given the resources. A key and vital resource is the network of social connections we take for granted.

THE GIFT OF CONNECTION

This is how the Little Way saves the world. On the surface, approaching people to form acquaintances and even surprising friendships doesn't seem like an effective way to help the poor. But when you realize the strength of weak ties, the Little Way becomes the exact intervention that can help the poor, creating and giving them a deeper and richer social network. As the research on concentrated poverty and social capital reveals, the poor don't need a handout;

they need better neighbors. And the Little Way gives them that.

And that's exactly how Beth got her new teeth.

Jana and I had been attending Freedom for a few months and had learned that, on Tuesday nights, the women of Freedom gathered for a meal and Bible study. Jana didn't know any of these ladies, but we'd been talking a lot about the Little Way, one of the main reasons we came to Freedom. Jana decided to approach. She didn't know anyone in the study, but she started going. And surprising friendships started to grow.

Many of the women in the study were poor like Beth. So when Beth shared her prayer request for new teeth, there was little the group could offer Beth other than prayer. But Jana had started attending the study, and she moved in a different social network. So the weak and strong ties Jana formed with the ladies in the class enriched their social capital. None of the ladies in the study knew any dentists. But Jana did.

Jana remembered Beth's request for teeth during her regular cleaning with our dentist. So Jana asked him a question: "How would you get someone some dentures at low cost?" He asked some questions, and Jana shared Beth's story and situation. Touched by her story, our dentist offered to fit Beth for dentures at cost, a few hundred dollars. That amount was well within the resources of Freedom. We shared with everyone at Freedom that if we all pitched in, we could get Beth some much-needed teeth. Everyone pitched in, and Beth got her teeth.

That's the strength of the weak tie. Beth didn't know a dentist, but Jana did; she had a weak tie with our dentist. And through that connection, a way was found to help Beth. Again, let's pay attention to the role of social connection in this story. Jana couldn't help Beth directly, since she's not a dentist. So when Jana first heard Beth's request, there was little she could do directly *for* Beth. And that's true for a lot of us. We make relationships with people, wanting to help and do things for them. But we are quickly overwhelmed with their needs and our lack of ability to decisively help. So we've formed a relationship, we've made a connection, but toward what end? It seems like, through the Little Way, we've sailed across this huge social sea to arrive and find that there's not a whole lot we can do to change people's lives.

Jana couldn't give Beth dental care, but Jana could give Beth and the Freedom community her social network. And that's all Freedom needed. That's the power of social capital. Suddenly we see the power of the early Christian experience of *koinonia.* The intimate fellowship of the early church wasn't there to reduce loneliness. *Koinonia* embedded the early Christians in a rich social network, exponentially increasing their social capital. The poor formed friendships with the rich. This network of relationships allowed the church to provide concrete and tangible care for each other, the same way Jana helped Freedom get Beth some new teeth.

But again, as we've seen throughout this book, this is a fragile business. Just as in our own time and place, the *koinonia* of the early church had to fight the social forces that pull our communities apart. The church had to overcome bias and racial prejudice. The early Christians had to do the hard work of confronting their own discrimination—how they privileged the wealthy and held prejudices against ethnic and racial groups.

So creating and enriching social networks is a hard and ongoing labor. That is why we need the Little Way, an intentional practice uniquely focused on moving us through the social and emotional barriers keeping us separated from each other.

When I think of Beth's new teeth, I'm reminded of how the Little Way saves the world. Through the Little Way, Jana made some surprising and unlikely friendships. And through the Little Way, Beth's prayers were finally answered.

CONCLUSION:
THE KINDNESS
REVOLUTION

In 2016, a man boarded a subway in Vancouver, Canada. He became aggressive, shouting and cursing at the other passengers. He jerked around erratically. The man was either mentally ill or under the influence of drugs. Everyone on the train backed away.

And then, suddenly, a seventy-year-old woman seated nearby reached out and held the hand of the shouting, cursing man. The gesture calmed him. The man quieted and then slumped to the ground, tears filling his eyes. The woman kept holding his hand. When he reached his stop, the man stood up and said, "Thanks, grandma." He exited and walked away.

Ehab Taha was on that train, and he took a picture of the old woman and the crazed man holding hands. He posted the picture to social media, and it quickly went viral. "It was quite incredible how much he calmed down in a split moment," Taha later said. "It was the most touching thing I've ever seen."[1]

Later in 2016, players from the Florida State University football team went to visit Tallahassee's Montford Middle School to spend time with area children. During the visit, the players ate lunch with the kids in the cafeteria. Travis Rudolph, a wide receiver for the Seminoles, spotted a child sitting off by himself, eating all alone in the crowded cafeteria. Travis approached the boy and asked if he could eat lunch with him. "Sure, why not?" the boy said. Travis sat down to have lunch with Bo Paske.

Bo was sitting alone, as he did most days, because he has autism. Witnessing Travis and Bo eating together, a friend of Bo's mother snapped a picture of the pair, and Bo's mother posted the picture to Facebook. The story and the picture went viral. Sharing the picture on Facebook Bo's mom wrote, "I'm not sure what exactly made this incredibly kind man share a lunch table with my son, but I'm happy to say that it will not soon be forgotten. This is one day I didn't have to worry if my sweet boy ate lunch alone."[2]

1. Rhianna Schmunk, "She Knew Exactly How to Comfort the 'Scary' Man on the SkyTrain," *Huffington Post*, February 5, 2016, http://www.huffingtonpost.ca/2016/02/04/skytrain_n_9161666.html.

These are just two stories of kindness among hundreds that captured our imaginations on social media. Kindness is viral. Perhaps it's because small acts of kindness are uncommon and rare. But I don't think that's the case. I think we're surrounded by small acts of kindness—gifts we give strangers and gifts we receive from them. No, I think these stories of kindness go viral because they remind us of who we want to be and they point the way to a better world.

I think it's time for Christians to give the word *love* a rest. Sure, we are called to love the world, even our enemies. And yes, love is supposed to be the quintessential Christian virtue. But love is such an overused word that we've lost touch with it. It's time to back up and focus on smaller, more practical, more basic stuff. Instead of trying to love the world, let's try practicing kindness. Because kindness is the tutor of love. Kindness is love on training wheels.

Or, as Thérèse puts it, kindness is the elevator to Jesus.

This call to focus on kindness over love might seem like I'm asking Christians to settle, like I'm

2. Jennifer Earl, "FSU Player Travis Rudolph Sits with Sixth-Grader with Autism Eating Lunch Alone," *CBS News*, August 31, 2016, http://www.cbsnews.com/news/fsu-player-travis-rudolph-sits-with-sixth-grade-boy-with-autism-eating-lunch-alone/.

suggesting that we trade in the hard, sacrificial thing—loving people—for something smaller and more trivial. But I think that focusing on the small and trivial just might be the revolution we've all been looking for.

Imagine what it would be like if Christians gave up trying to love the world for an entire year and instead committed ourselves to practicing kindness—kinder on social media, kinder with our coworkers, kinder with our family, kinder with our friends, kinder with everyone standing with us in line at the grocery store. I think a year of practicing kindness would revolutionize the Christian witness in the world.

We'd become a lot more loving in the process. Kindness isn't a spiritual ideal or aspiration; kindness is a *behavior* that causes you to lean in while others are leaning away. It's a behavior like taking the hand of a scary man on a subway, or eating lunch with someone who is sitting alone, or welcoming a woman in a hijab to your playgroup.

Kindness is what attracts us so much to Jesus. It's Jesus's kindness for those who have been treated meanly, cruelly, or dismissively. Our hearts thrill to the stories of kindness on social media because they remind us of Jesus. We see that seventy-year-old woman take the hand of a screaming crazy man, and we think of Jesus's kindness to those possessed by devils. We see the football player eating lunch with an autistic boy, and we think of Jesus touching lepers. We read these stories of kindness on social media, and our hearts leap in a flash of recognition: *That is exactly the sort of thing Jesus would have done.*

So maybe in all this Christian talk about love, we've set our sights too high. Maybe we'd be better able to welcome the stranger God if we got back to the smaller, humbler things. Hospitality—welcoming Jesus in disguise—begins with kindness, with widening the circle of our affections, living in the world as if there were no strangers. The spiritual discipline of the Little Way is simply the intentional practice of kindness.

So this is my final word of advice for those of us claiming to be followers of Jesus. If I were coaching us, this is what I'd tell my fellow Christians:

I think it's time to pull love out of the game. Let's let love take a seat on the bench to rest a bit and get a second wind. Let's erase the chalkboard and sketch out a new, simpler game plan to welcome the stranger God.

Let's start a kindness revolution.

A Note About the Cover

So, who is that man on the cover? Is that supposed to be Jesus, or someone else?

Both actually.

Brad Norr, the designer of the book cover, selected and used a picture of an unidentified homeless man to evoke the subtitle of the book, "Meeting Jesus in Disguise", and the book's central theme, finding Jesus in the eyes of a stranger.

Even in the eyes of a homeless man you'll pass on the street today.

I'm grateful for Brad's design. I hope that gaze on the cover will hauntingly remind us of Jesus's answer to the question—"When did we ever see you Lord?"—in Matthew 25:

"When I was a stranger, and you welcomed me."

ACKNOWLEDGMENTS

Thank you to the wonderful team at Fortress Press and Theology for the People for the opportunity to share this book.

A special thanks to Emily Sample and Rylee Schafer for their friendship and their hard work editing the manuscript.

Thank you to all the Men in White in the Monday-night Bible study at the French Robertson Unit and to all my family at Freedom Fellowship.

Finally, thank you to my wife, Jana. Jana has been my constant companion on our shared journey to live into Thérèse's Little Way. Plus, Jana has heard me present the material in this book to hundreds of people, over and over again. She never tires of it.

Jana and I have a joke that whenever I speak, I have only one message that I preach over and over again. As I head out the door to fly somewhere to speak again about hospitality, kindness, and the Little Way, Jana will say, "Tell them to be sweet like Jesus." I smile back and say, "I will."

Be sweet like Jesus.

If anyone has taught me how to do that, Jana, it's you.